SELECTED POEMS

Also by Donald Davie

Poems and Melodramas
To Scorch or Freeze
Collected Poems

Essays in Dissent
Older Masters
Slavic Excursions
Studies in Ezra Pound
Under Brigflatts

Donald Davie

Selected Poems

CARCANET

This edition published in 1997 by
Carcanet Press Limited
4th Floor, Conavon Court
12–16 Blackfriars Street
Manchester M3 5BQ

A CIP record for this book
is available from the British Library.
ISBN 1 85754 360 2

The publisher acknowledges financial assistance
from the Arts Council of England.

Printed and bound in England by SRP Ltd, Exeter.

Contents

from *Brides of Reason*

Evening on the Boyne   9
Poem as Abstract   10
Belfast on a Sunday Afternoon   11
The Garden Party   12
Pushkin. A Didactic Poem   13
Remembering the 'Thirties   15
The Evangelist   17
Method. For Ronald Gaskell   18

from *A Winter Talent*

Time Passing, Beloved   19
Dream Forest   19
The Mushroom Gatherers   20
The Wind at Penistone   21
The Priory of St Saviour, Glendalough   22
Samuel Beckett's Dublin   23
North Dublin   24
The Wearing of the Green   25
Mr Sharp in Florence   25
Via Portello   26
The Fountain   27
Hearing Russian Spoken   28
A Winter Talent   28
Gardens No Emblems   29
Rejoinder to a Critic   30
The Nonconformist   30
Heigh-ho on a Winter Afternoon   31

from *Poems of 1955-56*

Aubade   32
Dudwood   32

from *Forests of Lithuania*

"Who does not remember his Boyhood"   33
Epilogue   34

from *New & Selected Poems*

Against Confidences	34
To a Brother in the Mystery	35
With the Grain	37
The "Sculpture" of Rhyme	39

from *A Sequence for Francis Parkman*

Bougainville	40
A Letter to Curtis Bradford	41

from *Events & Wisdoms*

Resolutions	42
Life Encompassed	43
Hornet	44
Housekeeping	44
Low Lands	45
Green River	46
House-martin	46
The Prolific Spell	47
The Hill Field	48
A Lily at Noon	49
Across the Bay	50
In California	50
New York in August	51
In Chopin's Garden	52
Barnsley & District	53
Metals	55
Homage to John L. Stephens	55
The Hardness of Light	56

from *Poems of 1962-63*

Vying	57

from *Essex Poems*

Rodez	58
July 1964	59
January	60
Pietà	60

Sunburst	62
Ezra Pound in Pisa	63
Tunstall Forest	63
A Winter Landscape near Ely	64
Intervals in a Busy Life	65
Sylvae	65
Iowa	67
Back of Affluence	68
Or, Solitude	69

from *More Essex Poems*

My Father's Honour	70
Revulsion	71
Oak Openings	71
Democrats	72
Epistle. To Enrique Caracciolo Trejo	72
Cold Spring in Essex	74

from *Los Angeles Poems*

Christmas Syllabics for a Wife	75
"Abbeyforde"	76
Commodore Barry	77

from *The Shires*

Cheshire	79
Derbyshire	79
Nottinghamshire	80
Worcestershire	81
Yorkshire	81

from *In the Stopping Train*

Father, the Cavalier	83
The Harrow	84
The Departed	85
Rousseau in His Day	86
After the Calamitous Convoy	86
Seeing Her Leave	88
Portland	89

Ars Poetica   89
In the Stopping Train   91
Seur, near Blois   97
Morning   98
To a Teacher of French   99
Grudging Respect   100
A Spring Song   101

from *Three for Water Music*
Wild Boar Clough   102

from *The Battered Wife & Other Poems*
The Battered Wife   106
G.M.B. (10.7.77)   107
Short Run to Camborne   107
The Admiral to his Lady   108
Screech-Owl   109
Grace in the Fore Street   111
Ox-bow   112
No Epitaph   113
A Liverpool Epistle   114
Two from Ireland
    (1) Ireland of the Bombers   117
    (2) Near Mullingar   118
Devil on Ice   119
Advent   120
Having No Ear   122
Siloam   123

Evening on the Boyne

The Boyne at Navan swam in light,
Where children headlong through the trees
Plunged down the sward, and nicked the bright
Precarious evening with unease.

Swans at the bottom of a vale,
Sailing rapidly from sight,
Made the sweet arrangements fail
And emptied all the precious light.

A moment later all was well,
The light was full, the ranks were closed;
The fields of flags, the wading mill
Withdrew again, once more composed.

But what happened? Who had made
This mirror tremble and subside?
The evening by what eye betrayed
Winced, like a curtain drawn aside?

The shutter of some active mind,
Panicked by a glide of swans,
Closing, made all nature blind,
Then photographed itself at once.

O bleak and lunar emptiness,
How many eyes were then belied?
A god's, a man's, a swan's, and – yes,
The very flags were iris-eyed!

Poem as Abstract

"To write about a tree . . . you must first *be* a tree." (*W.R. Rodgers*)

I

A poem is less an orange than a grid;
It hoists a charge; it does not ooze a juice.
It has no rind, being entirely hard.

All drumming yards and open, it asserts
That clouds have way upon them, and that hills
Breast into time behind a singing strut.

A sheer abstraction, apt upon the grass
Of London parks, has emulated oak
And aped the ramage that it could surpass.

That construct, ribbed with wire across a quern,
Is caging such serenity of stress
As boughs, or fruit that breaks them, cannot learn.

For gods are gathered from the styles they wear,
And do they curl, a fœtus in a fruit,
Or, like Orion, pinned upon the air?

II

No trowelled matron but a rigger's mate,
The pile-high poet has no time to brood.
He steps the mast; it does not germinate.

Not for ingestion but to frame the air
He flies the spar that even winter's tree
In green ambition cannot grow so spare.

10

The orange dangles, drops, and comes again.
To make a fruit he has to be a fruit,
A globe of pulp about a pip of pain.

But tip-toe cages lofted in a day
(To make a grid he has to *make* a grid)
Have come unprecedented, and to stay.

If poems make a style, a way of walking
With enterprise, should not a poet's gait
Be counties-wide, this stride, the pylons stalking?

Belfast on a Sunday Afternoon

Visiting Belfast at the end of June,
We found the Orange Lodge behind a band:
Sashes and bearskins in the afternoon,
White cotton gloves upon a crippled hand.

Pastmasters pale, elaborately grim,
Marched each alone, beneath a bowler hat:
And, catapulted on a crumpled limb,
A lame man leapt the tram-lines like a bat.

And first of all we tried to laugh it off,
Acting bemusement in the grimy sun;
But stayed to worry where we came to scoff,
As loud contingents followed, one by one.

Pipe bands, flute bands, brass bands and silver bands,
Presbyter's pibroch and the deacon's serge,
Came stamping where the iron Mænad stands,
Victoria, glum upon a grassy verge.

11

Some brawny striplings sprawled upon the lawn;
No man is really crippled by his hates.
Yet I remembered with a sudden scorn
Those "passionate intensities" of Yeats.

The Garden Party

Above a stretch of still unravaged weald
In our Black Country, in a cedar-shade,
I found, shared out in tennis courts, a field
Where children of the local magnates played.

And I grew envious of their moneyed ease
In Scott Fitzgerald's unembarrassed vein.
Let prigs, I thought, fool others as they please,
I only wish I had my time again.

To crown a situation as contrived
As any in "The Beautiful and Damned",
The phantom of my earliest love arrived;
I shook absurdly as I shook her hand.

As dusk drew in on cultivated cries,
Faces hung pearls upon a cedar-bough;
And gin could blur the glitter of her eyes,
But it's too late to learn to tango now.

My father, of a more submissive school,
Remarks the rich themselves are always sad.
There is that sort of equalizing rule;
But theirs is all the youth we might have had.

Pushkin. *A Didactic Poem*

"he did not yet know well those hidden mechanisms of the person
by which it achieves its isolation from others and withdraws into
itself; he was entirely surrendered to his genius, disarmed by his
own power; and if his pride led him to challenge God, he cancelled
by that very act his own right to deny Him."   (*Wladimir Weidlé*)

What with hounds and friends and, in the winter,
Skating, he was seldom bored.
He had learned to be wary, was at pains, I think,
To remain amused?

In the matter of Pushkin, Emily Brontë
Is the best analogy in some ways
Among our poets. As in her verse,
In Pushkin's we assume the truth
That for life to be tolerable, man must
Be wary, ingenious, quick to change
Among diversions, grave or frivolous,
To keep off spleen; although for her,
As she was a woman, a narrower range
Presented itself, and so she is less
Various, flexible, fiery, though as noble
As Pushkin was, more stoical.

Pushkin's draughts-playing and his drinking,
His friends, his travelling, even some
Of his mistresses, he considered as
So many improvisations against
Boredom. But the boredom was
No vacancy nor want of occupation
Nor lack of resources. It was the spleen,

And Pushkin certainly fled before it
Or circumvented it. His poems
Record the circumventions as
Hours when the mind, turned outwards, knew
Friendships or the approach of death

13

As gifts. The poet exhibits here
How to be conscious in every direction
But that of the self, where deception starts.
This is nobility; not lost
Wholly perhaps, if lost to art.

Grateful tears, delicious sorrow,
Said the Russian gentleman,
Mozart will be dead tomorrow
Of this confusion.

As Byron said of Keats, "I don't
mean he is indecent, but
viciously soliciting
his own ideas."

(Schiller and Dostoievsky, oysters
Pearling their own disease, the saints
Full of self-help)

Long before Shakespeare wrote, or Donne,
In the modern manner, there were minds
Aware of themselves, and figuring this
In psychomachia. But the Greeks
Knew states of innocence, the will
Turned always outwards, courage the gift
Counting for virtue, and control,
As of the craven self, a notion
Lost in the social usage. Thus

Self-consciousness is not at fault
In itself. It can be kept
Other than morbid, under laws
Of disciplined sensibility, such
As the seventeenth-century Wit.
But all such disciplines depend
On disciplines of social use,
Now widely lost. Yet there are those

Few men remaining, gifted, or
Especially heroic, or,
Like Pushkin, brilliantly both.
Ask when we are diseased, and these
Will answer: When the moral will
Intervenes to sap the heart,
When the difficult feelings are
Titillated and confused
For novel combinations, or
Ransacked for virtue.

Remains the voice that moves on silence
In moral commonplace, where yet
Some thwart and stern communal sense
Whispers, before we all forget.

What need dissection of the thrust
Which motivates the skating feet,
When that can always be deduced
From the figure of eight?

What need dissection of the thrust
Which motivates the skating feet?
Skating with friends in the winter,
He foretold our defeat.

Remembering the 'Thirties

I

Hearing one saga, we enact the next.
We please our elders when we sit enthralled;
But then they're puzzled; and at last they're vexed
To have their youth so avidly recalled.

It dawns upon the veterans after all
That what for them were agonies, for us
Are high-brow thrillers, though historical;
And all their feats quite strictly fabulous.

This novel written fifteen years ago,
Set in my boyhood and my boyhood home,
These poems about "abandoned workings", show
Worlds more remote than Ithaca or Rome.

The Anschluss, Guernica – all the names
At which those poets thrilled or were afraid
For me mean schools and schoolmasters and games;
And in the process some-one is betrayed.

Ourselves perhaps. The Devil for a joke
Might carve his own initials on our desk,
And yet we'd miss the point because he spoke
An idiom too dated, Audenesque.

Ralegh's Guiana also killed his son.
A pretty pickle if we came to see
The tallest story really packed a gun,
The Telemachiad an Odyssey.

II

Even to them the tales were not so true
As not to be ridiculous as well;
The ironmaster met his Waterloo,
But Rider Haggard rode along the fell.

"Leave for Cape Wrath tonight!" They lounged away
On Fleming's trek or Isherwood's ascent.
England expected every man that day
To show his motives were ambivalent.

16

They played the fool, not to appear as fools
In time's long glass. A deprecating air
Disarmed, they thought, the jeers of later schools;
Yet irony itself is doctrinaire,

And, curiously, nothing now betrays
Their type to time's derision like this coy
Insistence on the quizzical, their craze
For showing Hector was a mother's boy.

A neutral tone is nowadays preferred.
And yet it may be better, if we must,
To praise a stance impressive and absurd
Than not to see the hero for the dust.

For courage is the vegetable king,
The sprig of all ontologies, the weed
That beards the slag-heap with his hectoring,
Whose green adventure is to run to seed.

The Evangelist

"My brethren . . ." And a bland, elastic smile
Basks on the mobile features of Dissent.
No hypocrite, you understand. The style
Befits a church that's based on sentiment.

Solicitations of a swirling gown,
The sudden vox humana, and the pause,
The expert orchestration of a frown
Deserve, no doubt, a murmur of applause.

The tides of feeling round me rise and sink;
Bunyan, however, found a place for wit.
Yes, I am more persuaded than I think;
Which is, perhaps, why I disparage it.

You round upon me, generously keen:
The man, you say, is patently sincere.
Because he is so eloquent, you mean?
That test was never patented, my dear.

If, when he plays upon our sympathies,
I'm pleased to be fastidious, and you
To be inspired, the vice in it is this:
Each does us credit, and we know it too.

Method. For Ronald Gaskell

For such a theme (atrocities) you find
My style, you say, too neat and self-possessed.
I ought to show a more disordered mind.

But Wesley's sermons could be methodized
According to a Ramist paradigm;
Enthusiasts can never be surprised.

The method in the madness of their zeal
Discounts their laceration of the wounds
That, though so bloodied, have had time to heal.

Cassandra plays her frenzied part too well
To be convincing in hysteria.
Has discourse still its several heads, in Hell?

It has, of course; and why conceal the fact?
An even tenor's sensitive to shock,
And stains spread furthest where the floor's not cracked.

Time Passing, Beloved

Time passing, and the memories of love
Coming back to me, carissima, no more mockingly
Than ever before; time passing, unslackening,
Unhastening, steadily; and no more
Bitterly, beloved, the memories of love
Coming into the shore.

How will it end? Time passing and our passages of love
As ever, beloved, blind
As ever before; time binding, unbinding
About us; and yet to remember
Never less chastening, nor the flame of love
Less like an ember.

What will become of us? Time
Passing, beloved, and we in a sealed
Assurance unassailed
By memory. How can it end,
This siege of a shore that no misgivings have steeled,
No doubts defend?

Dream Forest

These have I set up,
Types of ideal virtue,
To be authenticated
By no one's Life and Times,
But by a sculptor's logic

Of whom I have commanded,
To dignify my groves,
Busts in the antique manner,
Each in the space mown down
Under its own sway:

First, or to break the circle,
Brutus, imperious, curbed
Not much by the general will,
But by a will to be curbed,
A preference for limits;

Pushkin next, protean
Who recognised no checks
Yet brooked them all – a mind
Molten and thereby fluent,
Unforced, easily strict;

The next, less fortunate,
Went honourably mad,
The angry annalist
Of hearth and marriage bed,
Strindberg – a staring head.

Classic, romantic, realist,
These have I set up.
These have I set, and a few trees.
When will a grove grow over
This mile upon mile of moor?

The Mushroom Gatherers
after Mickiewicz

Strange walkers! See their processional
Perambulations under low boughs,
The birches white, and the green turf under.
These should be ghosts by moonlight wandering.

Their attitudes strange: the human tree
Slowly revolves on its bole. All around
Downcast looks; and the direct dreamer
Treads out in trance his lane, unwavering.

Strange decorum: so prodigal of bows,
Yet lost in thought and self-absorbed, they meet
Impassively, without acknowledgement.
A courteous nation, but unsociable.

Field full of folk, in their immunity
From human ills, crestfallen and serene.
Who would have thought these shades our lively friends?
Surely these acres are Elysian Fields.

The Wind at Penistone

The wind meets me at Penistone.
                            A hill
Curves empty through the township, on a slope
Not cruel, and yet steep enough to be,
Were it protracted, cruel.
                            In the street,
A plain-ness rather meagre than severe,
Affords, though quite unclassical, a vista
So bald as to be monumental.
                            Here
A lean young housewife meets me with the glance
I like to think that I can recognize
As dour, not cross.
                      And all the while the wind,
A royal catspaw, toying easily,
Flicks out of shadows from a tufted wrist,
Its mane, perhaps, this lemon-coloured sun.

The wind reserves, the hill reserves, the style
Of building houses on the hill reserves
A latent edge;
                  which we can do without
In Pennine gradients and the Pennine wind,

And never miss, or, missing it, applaud
The absence of the aquiline;
                        which in her
Whose style of living in the wind reserves
An edge to meet the wind's edge, we may miss
But without prejudice.
                    And yet in art
Where all is patent, and a latency
Is manifest or nothing, even I,
Liking to think I feel these sympathies,
Can hardly praise this clenched and muffled style.

For architecture asks a cleaner edge,
Is open-handed.
                And close-fisted people
Are mostly vulgar; only in the best,
Who draw, inflexible, upon reserves,
Is there a stern game that they play with life,
In which the rule is not to show one's hand
Until compelled.
               And then the lion's paw!
Art that is dour and leonine in the Alps
Grows kittenish, makes curios and clocks,
Giant at play.
             Here, nothing. So the wind
Meets me at Penistone, and, coming home,
The poet falls to special pleading, chilled
To find in Art no fellow but the wind.

The Priory of St Saviour, Glendalough

A carving on the jamb of an embrasure,
"Two birds affronted with a human head
Between their beaks" is said to be
"Uncertain in its significance but
A widely known design." I'm not surprised.

For the guidebook cheats: the green road it advises
In fact misled; and a ring of trees
Screened in the end the level knoll on which
St Saviour's, like a ruin on a raft,
Surged through the silence.

I burst through brambles, apprehensively
Crossed an enormous meadow. I was there.
Could holy ground be such a foreign place?
I climbed the wall, and shivered. There flew out
Two birds affronted by my human face.

Samuel Beckett's Dublin

When it is cold it stinks, and not till then.
The seasonable or more rabid heats
Of love and summer in some other cities
Unseal the all too human: not in his.
When it is cold it stinks, but not before;

Smells to high heaven then most creaturely
When it is cold. It stinks, but not before
His freezing eye has done its best to maim,
To amputate limbs, livelihood and name,
Abstracting life beyond all likelihood.

When it is cold it stinks, and not till then
Can it be fragrant. On canal and street,
Colder and colder, Murphy to Molloy,
The weather hardens round the Idiot Boy,
The gleeful hero of the long retreat.

When he is cold he stinks, but not before,
This living corpse. The existential weather
Smells out in these abortive minims, men
Who barely living therefore altogether
Live till they die; and sweetly smell till then.

North Dublin

St George's, Hardwicke Street,
Is charming in the Church of Ireland fashion:
The best of Geneva, the best of Lambeth
Aesthetically speaking
In its sumptuously sober
Interior, meet.

A continuous gallery, clear glass in the windows
An elegant conventicle
In the Ionian order –
What dissenter with taste
But would turn, on these terms
Episcopalian?

"Dissenter" and "tasteful" are contradictions
In terms, perhaps, and my fathers
Would ride again to the Boyne
Or with scythes to Sedgemoor, or splinter
The charming fanlights in this charming slum
By their lights, rightly.

The Wearing of the Green

Gold is not autumn's privilege;
A tawny ripening
In Meath in May burns ready in the hedge;
The yellow that will follow spring
Accentuates its wet and green array,
A sumptuous trill beneath
The shriller edge
Of Meath in May.

Green more entire must needs be evergreen,
Precluding autumn and this spring
Of Meath in May, its in-between
Of golds and yellows preluding
The liquid summer. Must the seasons stay
Their temperate career because
A flag is green
In Meath in May?

Imagination, Irish avatar,
Aches in the spring's heart and in mine, the stranger's,
In Meath in May. But to believe there are
Unchanging Springs endangers,
By that fast dye, the earth;
So blood-red green the season,
It never changes
In Meath in May.

Mr Sharp in Florence
"Mr Sharp from Sheffield, straight out of the knifebox."

Americans are innocents abroad;
But Sharp from Sheffield is the cagey kind
And – out of the knifebox, bleeding – can't afford
To bring to Florence such an open mind.

Poor Mr Sharp! And happy transatlantic
Travellers, so ingenuous! But some
Are so alert they can finesse the trick,
So strong they know when to be overcome.

Now must he always fall between these stools?
Blind, being keen; dumb, so as not to shrill;
Grounded and ground in logic-chopping schools;
So apt in so inapposite a skill?

Beleaguered and unsleeping sentinel,
He learned the trick of it, before the end;
Saw a shape move, and could not see it well,
Yet did not challenge, but himself cried, "Friend!"

Via Portello

"Nobody wants any more poems about . . . foreign cities."
Mr Kingsley Amis

Rococo compositions of decay,
Each a still-life, the fruity garbage-heaps
Teem by themselves. A broad and cobbled way,
Tiepolo's and Byron's thoroughfare
Lies grand and empty in its sullied air,
And watches while the rest of Padua sleeps.

The conscious vista closed at either end,
Here by a palace, that way by a gate
At night pure Piranesi . . . Yes, my friend,
I know you have decided for your part
That poems on foreign cities and their art
Are the privileged classes' shorthand. You must wait;

Or, traversing the colonnaded mile
Of this decayed locality, extend
The warmth of your resentment to the style
Of Padua's poor. A civilisation broken
Around them, theirs; and want, and no word spoken –
The conscious vista closed at either end.

The Fountain

Feathers up fast, and steeples; then in clods
Thuds into its first basin; thence as surf
Smokes up and hangs; irregularly slops
Into its second, tattered like a shawl;
There, chill as rain, stipples a danker green,
Where urgent tritons lob their heavy jets.

For Berkeley this was human thought, that mounts
From bland assumptions to inquiring skies,
There glints with wit, fumes into fancies, plays
With its negations, and at last descends,
As by a law of nature, to its bowl
Of thus enlightened but still common sense.

We who have no such confidence must gaze
With all the more affection on these forms,
These spires, these plumes, these calm reflections, these
Similitudes of surf and turf and shawl,
Graceful returns upon acceptances.
We ask of fountains only that they play,

Though that was not what Berkeley meant at all.

Hearing Russian Spoken

Unsettled again and hearing Russian spoken
I think of brokenness perversely planned
By Dostoievsky's debauchees; recall
The "visible brokenness" that is the token
Of the true believer; and connect it all
With speaking a language I cannot command.

If broken means unmusical I speak
Even in English brokenly, a man
Wretched enough, yet one who cannot borrow
Their hunger for indignity nor, weak,
Abet my weakness, drink to drown a sorrow
Or write in metres that I cannot scan.

Unsettled again at hearing Russian spoken,
"Abjure politic brokenness for good",
I tell myself. "Recall what menaces,
What self-loathings must be re-awoken:
This girl and that, and all your promises
Your pidgin that they too well understood "

Not just in Russian but in any tongue
Abandonment, morality's soubrette
Of lyrical surrender and excess,
Knows the weak endings equal to the strong;
She trades on broken English with success
And, disenchanted, I'm enamoured yet.

A Winter Talent

Lighting a spill late in the afternoon,
I am that coal whose heat it should unfix;
Winter is come again, and none too soon
For meditation on its raft of sticks.

Some quick bright talents can dispense with coals
And burn their boats continually, command
An unreflecting brightness that unrolls
Out of whatever firings come to hand.

What though less sunny spirits never turn
The dry detritus of an August hill
To dangerous glory? Better still to burn
Upon that gloom where all have felt a chill.

Gardens no Emblems

Man with a scythe: the torrent of his swing
Finds its own level; and is not hauled back
But gathers fluently, like water rising
Behind the watergates that close a lock.

The gardener eased his foot into a boot;
Which action like the mower's had its mould,
Being itself a sort of taking root,
Feeling for lodgement in the leather's fold.

But forms of thought move in another plane
Whose matrices no natural forms afford
Unless subjected to prodigious strain:
Say, light proceeding edgewise, like a sword.

Rejoinder to a Critic

You may be right: "How can I dare to feel?"
May be the only question I can pose,
"And haply by abstruse research to steal
From my own nature all the natural man"
My sole resource. And I do not suppose
That others may not have a better plan.

And yet I'll quote again, and gloss it too
(You know by now my liking for collage):
Donne could be daring, but he never knew,
When he inquired, "Who's injured by my love?"
Love's radio-active fall-out on a large
Expanse around the point it bursts above.

"Alas, alas, who's injured by my love?"
And recent history answers: Half Japan!
Not love, but hate? Well, both are versions of
The "feeling" that you dare me to . . . Be dumb!
Appear concerned only to make it scan!
How dare we now be anything but numb?

The Nonconformist

X, whom society's most mild command,
For instance evening dress, infuriates,
In art is seen confusingly to stand
For disciplined conformity, with Yeats.

Taxed to explain what this resentment is
He feels for small proprieties, it comes,
He likes to think, from old enormities
And keeps the faith with famous martyrdoms.

30

Yet it is likely, if indeed the crimes
His fathers suffered rankle in his blood,
That he finds least excusable the times
When they acceded, not when they withstood.

How else explain this bloody-minded bent
To kick against the prickings of the norm;
When to conform is easy, to dissent;
And when it is most difficult, conform?

Heigh-ho on a Winter Afternoon

There is a heigh-ho in these glowing coals
By which I sit wrapped in my overcoat
As if for a portrait by Whistler. And there is
A heigh-ho in the bird that noiselessly
Flew just now past my window, to alight
On winter's moulding, snow; and an alas,
A heigh-ho and a desultory chip,
Chip, chip on stone from somewhere down below.

Yes I have "mellowed", as you said I would,
And that's a heigh-ho too for any man;
Heigh-ho that means we fall short of alas
Which sprigs the grave of higher hopes than ours.
Yet heigh-ho too has its own luxuries,
And salts with courage to be jocular
Disreputable sweets of wistfulness,
By deprecation made presentable.

What should we do to rate the long alas
But skeeter down a steeper gradient?
And then some falls are still more fortunate,
The meteors spent, the tragic heroes stunned

Who go out like a light. But here the chip,
Chip, chip will flake the stone by slow degrees,
For hour on hour the fire will gutter down,
The bird will call at longer intervals.

Aubade

I wish for you that when you wake
You emulate the leaf and bird;
That like them, touched with grace, you take
Note of the wind. You have not heard
Its low-voiced billows yet, nor seen
(Lost in your less elated rest)
The empty light upon the green,
The leaves and tumbling birds that gave
The wind its due, and then redressed
That small excess, each bounding spray
A boat that dances on the wave,
A whip that tingles in the day.

Dudwood

The roads getting emptier, air in a steadily purer
Stream flowing back past the old Armstrong Siddeley tourer;
Then, the next morning, at large in the boulderstrewn
    woodland –
What worlds away from our nest in the chimney of England!
The turf carpets laid for us, scroll-like or star-shaped or
    trefoiled,
Deep pile to the tread of the spring-heel Jack Sparrows of
    Sheffield.

The bluff before Birchover, fronting the valley and shaded
By rowan and pine where the outcrop capped the precipitous
Comber of meadow. That way, in search of Cos lettuce
Or pony-tailed carrots, the three of us often ascended
That very first morning – all ardent and plumed, all cockaded
With springing abandonments, lost now, barely remembered.

"Who does not remember his Boyhood"

Who does not remember his boyhood, gun on shoulder,
    Whistling through unobstructed fields?
Overstepping the bounds, yet offending no leaseholder
    Of Lithuania, where the chase was free?

There ocean-goer, unmarked ship, the hunter
    Ranged at large; as augur,
Read skies and clouds; or to townsmen occult, an enchanter,
    Heard the earth-whisper.

Look in vain for the landrail, as lost down the meadow calling
    As pike in the Niemen, and look
In vain overhead for the lark whose carillon falling
    Around us rings in the Spring.

There an eagle wing rustles, appalling the sparrows,
    A comet dismaying the stars. And a falcon,
Fluttering butterfly pinned, when a hare moves in the meadow
    Stoops like a meteor.

When will the Lord God have us return, inhabit
    Ancestral fields, bear arms
Against the birds, and only to ride down the rabbit
    Muster our horse?

Epilogue

How many memories, what long sorrow
There where a man shall cleave to his master
As here no wife cleaves to her man;
There where a man grieves for loss of his weapons
Longer than here for who sired him;
And his tears fall more sincerely and faster
There for a hound than this people's for heroes.

My friends of those days made my speech come easy,
Each good for some singable idiom. Spring
Brought in the fable cranes of the wild island flying
Over the spellbound castle and the spellbound
Boy lamenting, who was loosed
By each pitying bird as it flew, one feather:
He flew out on those wings to his own people.

Against Confidences

Loose lips now
Call Candour friend
Whom Candour's brow,
When clear, contemned.

Candour can live
Within no shade
That our compulsive
Needs have made

On couches where
We sleep, confess,
Couple and share
A pleased distress.

34

Not to dispense
With privacies,
But reticence
His practice is;

Agreeing where
Is no denial,
Not to spare
One truth from trial,

But to respect
Conviction's plight
In Intellect's
Hard equal light.

Not to permit,
To shy belief
Too bleakly lit,
The shade's relief

Clouds Candour's brow,
But to indulge
These mouths that now
Divulge, divulge.

To a Brother in the Mystery
Circa 1290

The world of God has turned its two stone faces
One my way, one yours. Yet we change places
A little, slowly. After we had halved
The work between us, those grotesques I carved
There in the first bays clockwise from the door,
That was such work as I got credit for

At York and Beverley: thorn-leaves twined and bent
To frame some small and human incident
Domestic or of venery. Each time I crossed
Since then, however, underneath the vast
Span of our Mansfield limestone, to appraise
How you cut stone, my emulous hard gaze
Has got to know you as I know the stone
Where none but chisels talk for us. I have grown
Of my own way of thinking yet of yours,
Seeing your leafage burgeon there by the doors
With a light that, flickering, trenches the voussoir's line;
Learning your pre-harmonies, design
Nourished by exuberance, and fine-drawn
Severity that is tenderness, I have thought,
Looking at these last stalls that I have wrought
This side of the chapter's octagon, I find
No hand but mine at work, yet mine refined
By yours, and all the difference: my motif
Of foliate form, your godliness in leaf.
     And your last spandrel proves the debt incurred
Not all on the one side. There I see a bird
Pecks at your grapes, and after him a fowler,
A boy with a bow. Elsewhere, your leaves discover
Of late blank mask-like faces. We infect
Each other then, doubtless to good effect . . .
And yet, take care: this cordial knack bereaves
The mind of all its sympathy with leaves,
Even with stone. I would not take away
From your peculiar mastery, if I say
A sort of coldness is the core of it,
A sort of cruelty; that prerequisite
Perhaps I rob you of, and in exchange give
What? Vulgarity's prerogative,
Indulgence towards the frailties it indulges,
Humour called "wryness" that acknowledges
Its own complicity. I can keep in mind
So much at all events, can always find
Fallen humanity enough, in stone,

Yes, in the medium; where we cannot own
Crispness, compactness, elegance, but the feature
Seals it and signs it work of human nature
And fallen though redeemable. You, I fear,
Will find you bought humanity too dear
At the price of some light leaves, if you begin
To find your handling of them growing thin,
Insensitive, brittle. For the common touch,
Though it warms, coarsens. Never care so much
For leaves or people, but you care for stone
A little more. The medium is its own
Thing, and not all a medium, but the stuff
Of mountains; cruel, obdurate, and rough.

With the Grain

I

Why, by an ingrained habit, elevate
    Into their own ideas
Activities like carpentry, become
    The metaphors of graining?
Gardening, the one word, tilth? Or thought,
    The idea of having ideas,
Resolved into images of tilth and graining?

An ingrained habit . . . This is fanciful:
    And there's the rub
Bristling, where the irritable block
    Screams underneath the blade
Of love's demand, or in crimped and gouged-out
    Shavings only, looses
Under a peeling logic its perceptions.

Language (mine, when wounding,
        Yours, back-biting) lacks
No whorl nor one-way shelving. It resists,
        Screams its remonstrance, planes
Reluctantly to a level. And the most
        Reasonable of settlements betrays
Unsmoothed resentment under the caress.

II

The purest hue, let only the light be sufficient
        Turns colour. And I was told
If painters frequent St Ives
        It is because the light
There, under the cliff, is merciful. I dream
        Of an equable light upon words
And as painters paint in St Ives, the poets speaking.

Under that cliff we should say, my dear,
        Not what we mean, but what
The words would mean. We should speak,
        As carpenters work,
With the grain of our words. We should utter
        Unceasingly the hue of love
Safe from the battery of changeable light.

(Love, a condition of such fixed colour,
        Cornwall indeed, or Wales
Might foster. Lovers in mauve,
        Like white-robed Druids
Or the Bards in blue, would need
        A magical philtre, no less,
Like Iseult's, to change partners.)

III

Such a fourth estate of the realm,
        Hieratic unwinking
Mauve or blue under skies steel-silver,
        Would chamfer away

A knot in the grain of a streaming light, the glitter
    Off lances' points, that moved
A sluggish Froissart to aesthetic feeling.

And will the poet, carpenter of light,
    Work with the grain henceforward?
If glitterings won't fetch him
    Nor the refractory crystal,
Will he never again look into the source of light
    Aquiline, but fly
Always out of the sun, unseen till softly alighting?

Why, by an ingrained habit, elevate
    Into the light of ideas
The colourful trades, if not like Icarus
    To climb the beam? High lights
Are always white, but this ideal sun
    Dyes only more intensely, and we find
Enough cross-graining in the most abstract nature.

The "Sculpture" of Rhyme

    Potter nor iron-founder
Nor caster of bronze will he cherish,
    But the monumental mason;

    As if his higher stake
Than the impregnable spiders
    Of self-defended music

    Procured him mandibles
To chisel honey from the saxifrage,
    And a mouth to graze on feldspar.

Bougainville

Lewis de Bougainville, lieutenant to the Marquis of Montcalm at the fall of Canada, later essayed to annex the Falkland Islands.

Baulked of this object by the more politic arrangements of His Most Christian Majesty, his next and most extraordinary venture for the glory of the French nation was a circumnavigation of the globe in the years 1766, 1767, 1768 and 1769.

See his narrative of this voyage, made into English by Mr Forster; and the later extension of this work by the celebrated Diderot, a supplement more ingenious than useful.

All the soft runs of it, the tin-white gashes
Over the muscled mesh and interaction
Of the South Seas tilt against him less unsteady
Than France had been, or a King who could destroy
Acadia sold, Montcalm betrayed by faction,
And all the meadows of the Illinois
Lost, the allies abandoned. Where the ashes
Still smoulder on the ceded Falklands, these
Islands and oceans he has failed already
Though he will navigate the seven seas.

The shame persists as scruple. The exact
Conscience of science chastens observations,
And the redaction of a log-book's soundings
Is scrupulously dry. Although the scent
Carries from Otaheite, can a nation's
Chagrin or honour weigh in the intent
Scrutiny of the sextant? Matter of fact
Dries the great deeps. And yet what tumults when
He marks the fathoms, what disorders, houndings
Of mortification, angers, drive the pen!

No accuracy there but testifies
To a concern behind it, to a feeling
In excess of its object, fact. Excesses
Of that concern (where God permits the pox
And a King is perjured) self-inflict their steeling
To this impassive dryness charting rocks,

Keys, and the set of tide-rips. Weather eyes
Whittled so blue by pains, exactitude
In the science, navigation, witnesses
To the heart's intentions answered, not eschewed.

Needing to know is always how to learn;
Needing to see brings sightings; steadiest readings
Are those that wishes father. In their ages
Of Eden's gold the archipelagos
Await his keel because he wants for Edens
Who held savannahs once and the Ohio's
Bison for France. The measure of concern
Measures the truth, and in the *philosophe*
A paradox of noble savages
Has met no need more urgent than to scoff.

A Letter to Curtis Bradford

Curtis, you've been American too long,
You don't know what it feels like. You belong,
Don't you, too entirely to divulge?
Indifferently therefore you indulge
My idle interests: Are there names perhaps
In Iowa still, to match the names on maps,
Burgundian or Picard voyageurs
Prowling the wilderness for France and furs
On the Des Moines river? And suppose there were
What would it prove? To whom would it occur
In Iowa that, suppose it so, New France
Not your New England has pre-eminence
If to belong means anything? Your smile
(Twisted) admits it doesn't. Steadily, while
You on the seaboard, they in Canada
Dribbled from floods of European war

Boiled in small pools, pressure built up behind
The dams of Europe. Dispossessed mankind,
Your destined countrymen, milled at dock-gates;
Emigrant schooners spilled aboard the States;
The dispossessed, the not to be possessed,
The alone and equal, peopled all the West.
And so what is it I am asking for,
Sipping at names? Dahcotah, Ottawa,
Horse Indian . . . Yes, but earlier (What is this
Need that I find to fill void centuries?)
Who first put up America to let?
You of the old stock paid him rent. And yet
Even so soon, crowds of another sort
Piled off the boats to take him by assault.
And a worse sort, the heroes. Who but they,
For whom the manifest was shadow-play
Of an all-absorbing inward war and plight,
Could so deny its presence and its right?
It was the given. But I only guess,
I guess at it out of my Englishness
And envy you out of England. Man with man
Is all our history; American,
You met with spirits. Neither white nor red
The melancholy, disinherited
Spirit of mid-America, but this,
The manifested copiousness, the bounties.

Resolutions

Whenever I talk of my art
You turn away like strangers,
Whereas all I mean is the chart
I keep, of my own sea-changes.

It puzzles the wisest head
How anyone's good resolution
Can securely be implemented;
Art provides a solution.

This is the assessor whose word
Can always be relied on;
It tells you when has occurred
Any change you decide on.

More preciously still, it tells
Of growth not groped towards,
In the seaway a sound of bells
From a landfall not on the cards.

Life Encompassed

How often I have said,
"This will never do,"
Of ways of feeling that now
I trust in, and pursue!

Do traverses tramped in the past,
My own, criss-crossed as I forge
Across from another quarter
Speak of a life encompassed?

Well, life is not research.
No one asks you to map the terrain,
Only to get across it
In new ways, time and again.

How many such, even now,
I dismiss out of hand
As not to my purpose, not
Unknown, just unexamined.

Hornet

In lilac trained on the colonnade's archway, what
Must be a hornet volleys lethally back
And forth in the air, on the still not hot
But blindingly white Italian stone, blue-black.

I have seldom seen them in England, although once
Years ago the foul-mouthed, obligingly bowed
Rat-catcher of Cambridge made a just pretence
To a cup of tea, for a nest cleared in the road.

Those were wasp-coloured, surely; and this blue,
Gun-metal blue, blue-black ominous ranger
Of Italy's air means an Italy stone all through,
Where every herb of holier thought's a stranger.

No call for such rage in our England of pierced shadows.
Stone's and the white sun's opposite, furious fly,
There no sun strides in a rapid creak of cicadas
And the green mould stains before the mortar is dry.

Housekeeping

From thirty years back my grandmother with us boys
Picking the ash-grimed blackberries, pint on pint, is
Housekeeping Yorkshire's thrift, and yet the noise
Is taken up from Somerset in the 'nineties.

From homestead Autumns in the vale of Chard
Translated in youth past any hope of returning,
She toiled, my father a baby, through the hard
Fellside winters, to Barnsley, soused in the Dearne.

44

How the sound carries! Whatever the dried-out, lank
Sticks of poor trees could say of the slow slag stealing
More berries than we did, I hear her still down the bank
Slide, knickers in evidence, laughing, modestly squealing.

And I hear not only how homestead to small home echoes
Persistence of historic habit. Berries
Ask to be plucked, and attar pleases the rose.
Contentment cries from the distance. How it carries!

Low Lands

I could not live here, though I must and do
Ungratefully inhabit the Cambridgeshire fens
And the low river delta we pass through
Is beautiful in the same uncertain sense.

Like a snake it is, its serpentine iridescence
Of slow light spilt and wheeling over calm
Inundations, and a snake's still menace
Hooding with bruised sky belfry and lonely farm.

The grasses wave on meadows fat with foison.
In granges, cellars, granaries, the rat
Runs sleek and lissom. Tedium, a poison,
Swells in the sac for the hillborn, dwelling in the flat.

How defenceless it is! How much it needs a protector
To keep its dykes! At what a price it commands
The delightful bizarre when it wears like a bus-conductor
Tickets of brown sails tucked into polders' hat-bands!

But a beauty there is, noble, dependent, unshrinking,
In being at somebody's mercy, wide and alone.
I imagine a hillborn sculptor suddenly thinking
One could live well in a country short of stone.

Green River

Green silk, or a shot silk, blue
Verging to green at the edges,
The river reflects the sky
Alas. I wish that its hue
Were the constant green of its sedges
Or the reeds it is floating by.

It reflects the entrances, dangers,
Exploits, vivid reversals
Of weather over the days.
But it learns to make these changes
By too many long rehearsals
Of overcasts and greys.

So let it take its station
Less mutably. Put it to school
Not to the sky but the land.
This endless transformation,
Because it is beautiful,
Let some of it somehow stand.

But seeing the streak of it quiver
There in the distance, my eye
Is astonished and unbelieving.
It exclaims to itself for ever:
This water is passing by!
It arrives, and it is leaving!

House-martin

I see the low black wherry
Under the alders rock,
As the ferryman strides from his ferry
And his child in its black frock

Into his powerful shadow
And out of it, skirmishing, passes
Time and again as they go
Up through the tall lush grasses.

The light of evening grieves
For the stout house of a father,
With martins under its eaves,
That cracks and sags in the weather.

The Prolific Spell

Day by day, such rewards,
Compassionate land!
Such things to say, and the words
And ways of saying to hand!

Bounties I cannot earn!
Nothing planned in advance!
Well, it is hard to learn,
This profiting by chance.

It is hard, learning to live
While looking the other way,
Bored and contemplative
Over a child at play.

Not every one has a child.
All children grow away.
Sufferings drive us wild;
Not every mind can stray.

Nothing engendered, and so much
Constantly brought to birth!
This hand will lose its touch.
Profuse, illiberal earth!

Nothing could be planned
And so no credit accrues.
Ah compassionate land!
Such gain, and nothing to lose!

My utterance that turns
To always human use
Your brilliant mute concerns
Neither repays nor earns.

The Hill Field

Look there! What a wheaten
Half-loaf, halfway to bread,
A cornfield is, that is eaten
Away, and harvested:

How like a loaf, where the knife
Has cut and come again,
Jagged where the farmer's wife
Has served the farmer's men,

That steep field is, where the reaping
Has only just begun
On a wedge-shaped front, and the creeping
Steel edges glint in the sun.

See the cheese-like shape it is taking,
The sliced-off walls of the wheat
And the cheese-mite reapers making
Inroads there, in the heat?

It is Breughel or Samuel Palmer,
Some painter, coming between
My eye and the truth of a farmer,
So massively sculpts the scene.

The sickles of poets dazzle
These eyes that were filmed from birth;
And the miller comes with an easel
To grind the fruits of earth.

A Lily at Noon

Deep-sea frost, and
Lilies at noon . . .
Late leaves, late leaves
Toss every day.
The daymoon shines always for some.
In the marriage of a slow man
Eighteen years is soon.

Sun and moon, no
Dark between,
Foresight and hindsight
Halving the hours.
And now he collects his thoughts
Before it is too late.
But what can "too late" mean?

Shielding with hands,
Binding to stakes . . .
Late leaves, late leaves
Toss every day,
The sun moves on from noon.
To freeze, to cup, to retard –
These measures terror takes.

Across the Bay

A queer thing about those waters: there are no
Birds there, or hardly any.
I did not miss them, I do not remember
Missing them, or thinking it uncanny.

The beach so-called was a blinding splinter of limestone,
A quarry outraged by hulls.
We took pleasure in that: the emptiness, the hardness
Of the light, the silence, and the water's stillness.

But this was the setting for one of our murderous scenes.
This hurt, and goes on hurting:
The venomous soft jelly, the undersides.
We could stand the world if it were hard all over.

In California

Chemicals ripen the citrus;
There are rattlesnakes in the mountains,
And on the shoreline
Hygiene, inhuman caution.

Beef in cellophane
Tall as giraffes,
The orange-rancher's daughters
Crop their own groves, mistrustful.

Perpetual summer seems
Precarious on the littoral. We drive
Inland to prove
The risk we sense. At once

Winter claps-to like a shutter
High over the Ojai valley, and discloses
A double crisis,
Winter and Drought.

Ranges on mountain-ranges,
Empty, unwatered, crumbling,
Hot colours come at the eye.
It is too cold

For picnics at the trestle-tables. Claypit
Yellow burns on the distance.
The phantom walks
Everywhere, of intolerable heat.

At Ventucopa, elevation
Two-eight-nine-six, the water hydrant frozen,
Deserted or broken settlements,
Gasoline stations closed and boarded.

By nightfall, to the snows;
And over the mile on tilted
Mile of the mountain park
The bright cars hazarded.

New York in August
(after Pasternak)

There came, for lack of sleep,
A crosspatch, drained-out look
On the old trees that keep
Scents of Schiedam and the Hook

In Flushing, as we picked out, past
Each memorized landmark,
Our route to a somnolent breakfast.
Later, to Central Park,

UNO, and the Empire State.
A haven from the heat
Was the Planetarium. We got back late,
Buffeted, dragging our feet.

Clammy, electric, torrid,
The nights bring no relief
At the latitude of Madrid.
Never the stir of a leaf

Any night, as we went
Back, the children asleep,
To our bed in a loaned apartment,
Although I thought a deep

And savage cry from the park
Came once, as we flashed together
And the fan whirled in the dark,
For thunder, a break in the weather.

In Chopin's Garden

I remember the scarlet setts
Of the little-frequented highway
From Warsaw to the West
And Chopin's house, one Sunday.

I remember outside the windows,
As the pianist plucked a ring
From her thin white finger, the rows
Of unanchored faces waiting,

And a climbing vapour, storm-wrack
Wreathing up, heavy with fruit,
Darkened the skies at their back
On the old invasion-route.

Masovia bows its birches
Resignedly. Again
A rapid army marches
Eastward over the plain,

And fast now it approaches.
Turbulence, agonies,
As the poised musician broaches
The polonaise, storm from the keys.

See them, ennobled by
The mass and passage, these
Faces stained with the sky,
Supple and fluid as trees.

Barnsley and District

Judy Sugden! Judy, I made you caper
With rage when I said that the British Fascist
Sheet your father sold was a jolly good paper

And you had agreed and I said, Yes, it holds
Vinegar, and everyone laughed and imagined
The feel of the fish and chips warm in its folds.

That was at Hood Green. Under our feet there shone
The modest view, its slagheaps amethyst
In distance and white walls the sunlight flashed on.

If your father's friends had succeeded, or if I
Had canvassed harder for the Peace Pledge Union,
A world of difference might have leapt to the eye

In a scene like this which shows in fact no change.
That must have been the summer of '39.
I go back sometimes, and find nothing strange –

Short-circuiting of politics engages
The Grammar School masters still. Their bright sixth-formers sport
Nuclear Disarmament badges.

And though at Stainborough no bird's-nesting boy
Nor trespasser from the town in a Sunday suit
Nor father twirling a stick can now enjoy

Meeting old Captain Wentworth, who in grey
And ancient tweeds, gun under arm, keen-eyed
And unemployable, would give a gruff Good-day,

His rhododendrons and his laurel hedge
And tussocked acres are no more unkempt
Now that the hall is a Teachers' Training College.

The parish primary school where a mistress once
Had every little Dissenter stand on the bench
With hands on head, to make him out a dunce;

Blank backs of flourmills, wafer-rusted railings
Where I ran and ran from colliers' boys in jerseys,
Wearing a blouse to show my finer feelings –

These still stand. And Bethel and Zion Baptist,
Sootblack on pavements foul with miners' spittle
And late-night spew and violence, persist.

George Arliss was on at the Star, and Janet Gaynor
Billed at the Alhambra, but the warmth
Was no more real then, nor the manners plainer.

And politics has no landscape. The Silesian
Seam crops out in prospects felt as deeply
As any of these, with as much or as little reason.

Metals

Behind the hills, from the city of an Etruscan gateway
To the city of a Sienese fortress
Through the metalliferous mountains,
If I had travelled to the age of bronze,
Of gold, the pierced axe-heads of archaic Greece,
This would have been my way.

For first we corkscrewed in a stink of borax
For climbing miles, then under the oakwoods
In unworked lodes lay poisonous zinc and copper.
With forty miles to go, the car bit gravel
Which spurted and hung in the air, and still no houses.

And I saw all stone as a weak concoction of powder,
The golden skin of the columns
Cemented as limply as a Rizla paper.
Rape may be worship. Where the sybil stands
In a pool of spent light at the heart of the mountain at Cumae,
The bowels of earth are of an unearthly weirdness.

Homage to John L. Stephens

There has to be a hero who is not
A predator but South
Of the Border down
Mexico way or wherever else she
Whispers, It's best not to linger.

Fever: bright starlight, and the sails
Flapping against the mast, the ocean
Glass, and the coastline dark,
Irregular, and portentous with volcanoes;
The Great Bear almost upon him, the North Star
Lower than ever, waning as he was waning,

And not that sort of hero, not
Conquistador Aeneas, but a tourist!
Uncoverer of the Maya, John L. Stephens,
Blest after all those beaks and prows and horses.

The Hardness of Light

"Via Portello," I wrote,
"The fruity garbage-heaps . . ."
As if someone had read my poems,
Padua eight years later
Is so hot no one sleeps.

But this is a different quarter,
Just off the *autostrada*,
Touched by that wand of transit,
Californian, hopeful . . .
I grow older, harder.

I wake in the night, to rain.
All the old stench released
On the risen night wind carries
Coolness across the city,
Streaming from west to east.

The equivocal breath of change,
In a clatter of sudden slats
Across the room, disturbs me
More than ever, in new
Motels and blocks of flats.

What is this abomination
When a long hot spell is breaking?
Sour smell of my own relief?
The rankness of cooling-off?
Rottenness of forsaking?

I glare. In that renowned
Hard light of burning skies
Nothing grows durable
With age. It neither solves
Nor even simplifies.

Vying

Vying is our trouble;
And a devious vice it is
When we vie in abnegations,
Services, sacrifices.

Not to be devious now
(For perhaps I should not begin
Taking the blame for winning
If this were not how to win),

I assert that such is the case:
I seem to have more resources;
I thrive on enforcing the more
The less naked the force is.

Mutinies, sulks, reprisals
All play into my hand;
To be injured and forgiving
Was one of the roles I planned.

Married to me, you take
The station I command,
As if in a peopled graveyard
Deserted in an upland.

There I, the sexton, battle
Earth that will overturn
Headstones, and rifle tombs,
And spill the tilted urn.

Rodez

Northward I came, and knocked in the coated wall
At the door of a low inn scaled like a urinal
With greenish tiles. The door gave, and I came

Home to the stone north, every wynd and snicket
Known to me wherever the flattened cat
Squirmed home to a hole between housewall and paving.

Known! And in the turns of it, no welcome,
No flattery of the beckoned lighted eye
From a Rose of the rose-brick alleys of Toulouse.

Those more than tinsel garlands, more than masks,
Unfading wreaths of ancient summers, I
Sternly cast off. A stern eye is the graceless

Bulk and bruise that at the steep uphill
Confronts me with its drained-of-colour sandstone
Implacably. The Church. It is Good Friday.

Goodbye to the Middle Ages! Although some
Think that I enter them, those centuries
Of monkish superstition, here I leave them

With their true garlands, and their honest masks,
Every fresh flower cast on the porch and trodden,
Raked by the wind at the Church door on this Friday.

Goodbye to all the centuries. There is
No home in them, much as the dip and turn
Of an honest alley charmingly deceive us.

And yet not quite goodbye. Instead almost
Welcome, I said. Bleak equal centuries
Crowded the porch to be deflowered, crowned.

July, 1964

I smell a smell of death.
Roethke, who died last year
with whom I drank in London,
wrote the book I am reading;
a friend, of a firm mind,
has died or is dying now,
a telegram informs me;
the wife of a neighbour died
in three quick months of cancer.

Love and art I practise;
they seem to be worth no more
and no less than they were.
The firm mind practised neither.
It practised charity
vocationally and
yet for the most part truly.
Roethke, who practised both,
was slack in his art by the end.

The practice of an art
is to convert all terms
into the terms of art.
By the end of the third stanza
death is a smell no longer;
it is a problem of style.
A man who ought to know me
wrote in a review
my emotional life was meagre.

January

Arable acres heave
Mud and a few bare trees
Behind St Michael's
Kirby le Soken, where
The pew I share
Promises the vicinity I leave.

Diatribe and
Denunciation, where
I spend my days,
Populous townships, sink
Into the haze that lowers
Over my neighbour's land.

Resignation, oh winter tree
At peace, at peace . . .
Read it what way you will,
A wish that fathers. In a field between
The Sokens, Thorpe and Kirby, stands
A bare Epiphany.

Pietà

Snow-white ray
coal-black earth will
swallow now.
The heaven glows
when twilight has
kissed it, but
your white face
which I kiss now does
not. Be still

acacia boughs,
I talk with my
dead one. We speak
softly. Be still.

The sky is blind
with white
cloud behind
the swooping birds. The
garden lies
round us and
birds in the dead
tree's bare
boughs shut
and open themselves. Be
still, or be
your unstill selves,
birds in the tree.

The wind is
grievous to the willow. The
underside of its
leaves as the wind
compels them is
ashen. Bow
never, nor dance
willow. How can
you bear it? My
head goes back on
my neck fighting
the pain off. Willow
in the wind, share it.

I have to learn
how time can be
passed in public
gardens. There my

dead lies idle. Much
bereaved and sitting
under a sunny wall
old women stare
through me. I
come too soon and
yet at last to
fixity, being alone and
with a crone's pastimes.

In memoriam Douglas Brown

Sunburst

The light wheels and comes in
over the seawall
and the bitten turf
that not only wind has scathed but
all this wheeling and flashing, this
sunburst comes across us.

At Holland on Sea
at an angle from here and
some miles distant
a fisherman reels back blinded,
a walker is sliced in two.
The silver disc came at them
edgewise, seconds ago.

Light that robes us, does it?
Limply, as robes do, moulded
to the frame of Nature? It
has no furious virtue?

Ezra Pound in Pisa

Excellence is sparse.
I am made of a Japanese mind
Concerning excellence:
However sparred or fierce
The furzy elements,
Let them be but few
And spaciously dispersed,
And excellence appears.

Not beauty. As for beauty,
That is a special thing.
Excellence is what
A man who treads a path
In a prison-yard might string
Together, day by day,
From straws blown in his path
And bits of remembering.

Sun moves, and the shadow moves,
In spare and excellent order;
I too would once repair
Most afternoons to a pierced
Shadow on gravelly ground,
Write at a flaked, green-painted
Table, and scrape my chair
As sun and shade moved round.

Tunstall Forest

Stillness! Down the dripping ride,
    The firebreak avenue
Of Tunstall Forest, at the side
    Of which we sought for you,

You did not come. The soft rain dropped,
    And quiet indeed we found:
No cars but ours, and ours was stopped,
    Rainfall the only sound.

And quiet is a lovely essence;
    Silence is of the tomb,
Austere though happy; but the tense
    Stillness did not come,
The deer did not, although they fed
    Perhaps nearby that day,
The liquid eye and elegant head
    No more than a mile away.

A Winter Landscape near Ely

It is not life being short,
Death certain, that is making
Those faintly coffee-coloured
Gridiron marks on the snow
Or that row of trees heart-breaking.

What stirs us when a curtain
Of ice-hail dashes the window?
It is the wasteness of space
That a man drives wagons into
Or plants his windbreak in.

Spaces stop time from hurting.
Over verst on verst of Russia
Are lime-tree avenues.

Intervals in a Busy Life

"Room for manœuvre," I say,
"I ask for an undertaking."
Manœuvring, king-making . . .

Only when death happens
Do I see the tops of the trees
Out of my attic window,

And they are always there:
They have looked on the death of my friend
And on my father's death.

They are the deathly markers;
And thereby, even when leafless,
Green; ungrudging sources

At which, as at holy springs,
One does not drink
Habitually nor lightly.

Filling the intervals
Without propriety
Itself is reverential.

Sylvae

Not deerpark, royal chase,
Forest of Dean, of Windsor,
Not Cranborne, Savernake
Nor Sherwood nor that old
Plantation we can call
New, nor be, it is
So old, misunderstood;
But the primordial oak-wood.

This it is our hedgerows
Preserve from the pre-Saxon:
Not the perennial pastures;
Not Hanoverian georgics;
But a prodigious dapple
Of once uninterrupted
Cover we at best
Subvert by calling "forest".

Sprung of this cultured landscape
The fiction-makers of
My race have so completely
Made over it escapes
Nowhere from that old love,
Conniving at reversion
I think of Robin Hood,
The flecked man in my blood.

I think how the tractable Nature
Of the cultivator has
Before now, at the hand
Of many a bookish writer,
Burgeoned in garden-crops
By seasons, and he has
Made homage of them for
Patron or paramour.

But I have kept no gardens,
Am of that vanquished sort,
The gatherers, the most
Primitive of woodland cultures;
I have to offer her
To whom I most would make
Offer, no more than nuts,
Berries, and dubious roots.

Iowa

The blanched tree livid behind
The smaller conifer
Looks to be entangled with it.

Dutch elm disease is in town,
Carried by worms from the eastern seaboard
Twelve hundred miles.

Gesticulating down
And around, emaciated,
This is the many-armed,

This is the elephant-headed
Ganesh of good beginnings,
God of the Hindu, gone sick.

Tomorrow, if the night is warmer,
The snow will be gone in patches
From the clay-spoil hillock.

White on white, a white
Framehouse amid the snow
Is a peculiar beauty.

The tree is an ivory colour.
In a white world there are
So many kinds of white.

They leak into black shadows
Draining them blue. I shall be
Sorry when the world goes piebald.

Red on red was a good chequer,
The red man dead in his blood;
And black on black, the weighed bough swinging

In a night of Alabama. White on white
Is a man of my colour, sick,
Falling down in the snow.

Back of Affluence

That time of the early year
When the sun has a head of hair
Crisp but growing out,
When already the long nights have
Stirred away southward, when
The engraver frost still makes
Likenesses of his sister
Snow, but with a nib
That will not hold its point,

Then the Iowan farmer,
His fodder low, looked out
And saw the prairie white.

He threw up a heavy arm,
He stamped in the house at a loss.
His wife rose lame and stiff.
His children snarled like dogs.

Then he came back with the team;
She into her best dress
Wrinkled at waist and shoulder.
No farming, a day on the town!
Rail depot through to horsepond
And lumberyard, one street.
She with a child in arms;
No place to go from the wind.

Some one has said that it
Brutalized. It did,
That poverty. And what she
Could have seen, she had not
The ease of heart to see:
The sun like a Chinese brush
Writing in delicate shadow
"Tree" on a framehouse front;
The handsomely carpentered boards
Fanned across, splayed over
With a serene springing.

Or, Solitude

A farm boy lost in the snow
Rides his good horse, Madrone,
Through Iowan snows for ever
And is called "alone".

Because gone from the land
Are the boys who knew it best
Or best expressed it, gone
To Boston or Out West,

And the breed of the horse Madrone,
With its bronco strain, is strange
To the broken sod of Iowa
That used to be its range,

The metaphysicality
Of poetry, how I need it!
And yet it was for years
What I refused to credit.

69

My Father's Honour

Dim in the glimmering room
Over against my bed . . .
Astonished awake, I held
My breath to see my dead,
My green-eyed, talkative
Dead father come.

That look he has! A rare one
In a vivacious man.
I grasp at the uncommon
Identifiable look,
Reproach. The charge it levels
Is no unfair one.

Hold to that guise, reproach,
Cat's eyes! Eerily glow,
Green, prominent, liquid;
Level the charge, although
I could not have done other,
And this you know.

Hold there, green eyes! But no,
Upon the nebulous ground
His merciful nature cuts
From shot to genial shot,
Indulgent now, as if
In honour bound.

Revulsion

Angry and ashamed at
Having not to look,
I have lived constricted
Among occasions
Of nausea, like this book
That I carefully leave on the train.

My strongest feeling all
My life has been,
I recognize, revulsion
From the obscene;
That more than anything
My life-consuming passion.

That so much more reaction
Than action should have swayed
My life and rhymes
Must be the heaviest charge
That can be brought against
Me, or my times.

Oak Openings

The "I have" poem
(Have been, seen, done)
Is followed by the "What about it?" poem.
There is plenty new under the sun,
This poem says, but what's
So new about the new?

It is not as if the attention
Steadily encroaches
Upon the encircling dark;
The circle about the torch is
Moving, it opens new
Glades by obscuring old ones.

Twigs crack under foot, as the tread
Changes. The forge-ahead style
Of our earliest ventures flags;
It becomes, as mile follows mile
Inexhaustibly, an exhausted
Wavering trudge, the explorer's.

Democrats

Four close but several trees, each green, none equal.
They are the glory of this countryside:
Sequestered households of the field and hedge,
Not copses and not spinneys and not groves.

Green and uncertain in the early summer;
Patient endurers down the depth of winter,
Immobile dancers. In these fields the axe
Of the leveller Tarquin trembles, and advances.

Epistle. To Enrique Caracciolo Trejo
(Essex)

A shrunken world
Stares from my pages.
What a pellet the authentic is!
My world of poetry,
Enrique, is not large.

Day by day it is smaller.
These poems that you have
Given me, I might
Have made them English once.
Now they are inessential.
The English that I feel in
Fears the inauthentic
Which invades it on all sides
Mortally. The style may die of it,
Die of the fear of it,
Confounding authenticity with essence.

Death, an authentic subject,
Jaime Sabinès has
Dressed with the yew-trees of funereal trope.
It cannot be his fault
If the English that I feel in
Feels itself too poor
Spirited to plant a single cypress.
It is afraid of showing, at the grave-side,
Its incapacity to venerate
Life, or the going of it. These are deaths,
These qualms and horrors shade the ancestral ground.

Sabinès in another
Poem comes down
To the sound of pigeons on a neighbour's tiles,
A manifest of gladness.
Such a descent on clapping wings the English
Contrives to trust
No longer. My own garden
Crawls with a kind of obese
Pigeon from Belgium; they burst through cracking branches
Like frigate-birds.

Still in infested gardens
The year goes round,
A smiling landscape greets returning Spring.
To see what can be said for it, on what
Secure if shallow ground
Of feeling England stands
Unshaken for
Her measure to be taken
Has taken four bad years
Of my life here. And now
I know the ground:
Humiliation, corporate and private,
Not chastens but chastises
This English and this verse.

I cannot abide the new
Absurdities day by day,
The new adulterations.
I relish your condition,
Expatriate! though it be among
A people whose constricted idiom
Cannot embrace the poets you thought to bring them.

Cold Spring in Essex

Small boy in a black hat walks among streaky shadows
Under my window, and I am at ease this morning.
This day reminds me of Budapest. All over
Europe is the North and Protestantism has conquered.

The Roman Catholic North in the black-oak cabinet of Antwerp
Is an irreplaceable grace-note, as at Sawston
The manorial chapel of the Huddlestons for the pilgrims.
"Which of them will make a good death?" my friend in Antwerp
Wondered through the plateglass over beer and coffee

Looking to the end.
                        But I am happy this morning,
Looking into my garden, seeing the cold light standing
Oblique to the grey-green tree-trunks and the grasses,
All over my illimitable future.

Christmas Syllabics for a Wife

When I think of you
dying before or
after me, I am
ashamed how little
there is for either
one of us to look
back upon as done
wholly in concert.

We have spent our lives
arming for them. Now
we see they begin
to be over, and
now is it too late
to profit by what
seems to have been a
long preparation?

The certainty that
many have scaped scot-
free or even praised
sets the adrenalin
anger flushing up
through me as often
before, but can we
wait now for justice?

Horace says, Be wise
broach the ripe wine and
carefully decant
it. Now is the time
to measure wishes
by what life has to
give. Not much. So be
from now on greedy.

"Abbeyforde"

Thirty years unremembered,
Monkey-faced black-bead-silken
Great-aunt I sat across from,
Gaping and apprehensive,
The thought of you suddenly fits.
Across great distances
Clement time brings in its
Amnesties, Aunt Em.

"Abbeyforde": the name
Decyphered stood for Ford
Abbey, in Somerset. There
Your brother's sweetheart Nell,
My grandmother, drew him to her,
Whom later he pitchforked North.
Such dissolutions, Em!
Such fatal distances!

"Keep still feast for ever . . ."
A glow comes up off the page
In which I read of a paschal
Feast of the diaspora

In Italy, in a bad
Time for the Jews, and it is
As if in that tender and sad
Light your face were illumined.

Commodore Barry

When Owen Roe
O'Sullivan sang Ho
For the hearts of oak
Of broken Thomond, though
Weevils and buggery should
Have wormed the wooden walls
More than De Grasse's cannon,
The sweetest of the masters
Of Gaelic verse in his time,
Lame rhymester in English, served
And laurelled Rodney's gun.

Available as ever
Implausibly, the Stuart
Claimed from the Roman stews
His sovereignty *de jure*;
But Paddy, in the packed
Orlop, the *de facto*
Sovereignty of ordure,
King George's, had to hedge
His bet upon a press
Of white legitimist sail
Off Kinsale, some morning.

A flurry of whitecaps off
The capes of the Delaware!
Barry, the Irish stud,
Has fathered the entire

American navy! Tories
Ashore pore over the stud-book,
Looking in vain for the mare,
Sovran, whom Jolly Roger
Of Wexford or Kildare
Claims in unnatural congress
He has made big with frigates.

Loyalists rate John
Paul Jones and Barry, traitors;
One Scotch, one Irish, pirate.
In Catherine the Great's
Navy, her British captains
Years later refused to sail with
The Scot-free renegade. Jones
And Barry took the plunge
Right, when the sovereigns spun;
Plenty of Irish pluck
Called wrong, was not so lucky.

"*My* sovereign," said saucy
Jack Barry, meaning Congress;
And yes, it's true, outside
The untried, unstable recess
Of the classroom, every one has one:
A sovereign – general issue,
Like the identity-disc,
The prophylactic, the iron
Rations. Irony fails us,
Butters no parsnips, brails
No sail on a ship of the line.

Cheshire

A lift to the spirit, when everything fell into place!
So that was what those ruined towers remained from:
Engine-houses, mills. Our Pennine crests
Had not been always mere unfettered space.

Not quite the crests, just under them. The high
Cloughs, I learned in the history-lesson, had
Belted the earliest mills, they had connived
With history then, then history passed them by.

His savage brunt and impetus, one survives it?
Finding it all unchanged and the windowless mill
Between Wincle and Congleton silent and staring, I found
The widow's weeds restorative and fit.

And Mr Auden, whom I never knew,
Is dead in Vienna. A post-industrial landscape
He celebrated often, and expounded
How it can bleakly solace. And that's true.

Derbyshire

We never made it. Time and time again
Sublimity went unexamined when
We turned back home through Winster, lacking heart
For walking further. Yet the Romantic part
Of Via Gellia, where it dives through chasms
To Ashbourne, is historic; there, short spasms
Of horror once in many a heaving breast
Gave Derbyshire a dreadful interest.

79

And I too was Romantic when I strode
Manfully, aged 12, the upland road.
Only the name of "Via Gellia" jarred;
It seemed to mean a classical boulevard
With belvederes at intervals. I swelled
My little chest disdainfully, I "rebelled"!

Nottinghamshire

Rosebay willow herb pushing
through patches of old slag
in the curtains of driving rain
obscured the Major Oak.

Or else (our steam was blurring
the windows of the Hillman)
it was our being hounded
out of doors that felled
the last tall stands of Sherwood.

Robin of Locksley, Guy
of Gisborne, and the Sheriff
of Nottingham had been dapples
under my mother's smiles
all down the glades of boyhood.

But now she could take no more
of us, and of our baby.

In the country of Sons and Lovers
we think we know all too much
about the love of mothers.

Angry and defiant,
rash on industrial waste,
the rosebay willow herb
is, of all the flowers
she taught me, one I remember.

Worcestershire

for Doreen

The best way in (not that I've checked the map)
Might be from West by North, as once we came
After a drive through spooky Radnor Forest
Where you had sat upon a picnic rug
And wept and wept. I laboured into verse
My sense of that, and made no sense at all.

Maria Theresa, I addressed you as,
Imperial sorrow. God knows what I meant
By that, or thought I meant. If I could not
Make you Fair Austria then, I shall not now;
But spin you down, down by whatever stages
Wise maps might tell me, into the blossoming plains.

Feed you with apples, stay you with flagons, Empress!
Acre on acre of orchards of Worcester Pearmains!

Yorkshire

Of Graces

The graces, yes – and the airs! To airs and graces
Equally the West Riding gave no houseroom
When I was young. Ballooning and mincing airs
Put on in the "down there" of England! I was
Already out of place in the heraldic
Cities of the Midlands – Warwick, Leicester, the South . . .

  – And therefore it is a strain, thinking of Brough
  And Appleby gone from King John to a Frenchman
  For dirty work done on the roads of Poitou.

This helps me – not to pipe like your reed, Bunting,
Master of Northern stops – but to remember,
Never quite well enough, Kirkby Stephen
By Aisgill on to Hawes, to Aysgarth, Askrigg,
The narrow dale past a hump of broken stones.
Slant light out of Lancashire burnished the fell.

Alix, Kate, Eleanor, Anne – Angevin names –
You were not my hopscotch-mates; but Rhoda,
Thelma and Mona. Enormous their mottled
Fore-arms drove flat-irons later, strove with sheets
In old steam-laundries. There the Saxons queened it
No less – the Elfridas, Enids, many Hildas.

Ladies, ladies! Shirley or Diane or . . .
Which of you girls will be mine? Which of you all
In my dishonourable dreams sits smiling
Alone, at dusk, and knowledgeably sidelong,
Perched on a heap of stones, where "Dangerous" says
The leaning board, on a green hill south of Brough?

Where is the elf-queen? Where the beldam Belle Dame?
Feyness of the North, kelpie of some small beck
In a swale of marble swirls over Durham,
Irrigates Elmet, combs the peat in Ewden.
And I have no faith in that: *le fay* thinned out
Into a pulse in the grass, St Winifred.

Eleanor rather, Alix, ladies of Latins,
I call you down. (And Mary, Mother of Heaven?)
Justice and Prudence (Prue, a name not given
North of the Trent), Courage, and Temperance were
Your erudite names, mothers of Latin earth.
What *royaume* of earth, elf-queen, did you sway ever?

Charites or *Gratiae*, the Graces,
Lemprière says, "presided over kindness",
Each dam in her own kind fructive. Only two.
(Three came later.) Two: *Hegemone*, the Queen,
And *Auxo*, Increase. Queen of Elfland, in what
Assize did you sit, what increase ever foster?

Now every girl has this elvish admixture.
Thomas of Ercildoune, what you dreamed of once
Fogs every brae-side: lank black the hair hangs down,
The curves of the cheek are hollow and ravaged.
Their womanhood a problematic burden
To them and their castrated mates, they go past.

I have a Grace. Whether or no the Muses
Patronize me, I have a Grace in my house
And no elf-lady. Queen she is called, and Increase,
Though late-come, straitened, of a Northern Province.

Father, the Cavalier

I have a photograph here
    In California where
You never were, of yourself
    Riding a white horse. And
The horse and you are dead
    Years ago, although
Still you are more alive
    To me than anyone living.

As for the horse: an ugly
    Wall-eyed brute, apparently
Biddable though, for I cannot
    Believe you were ever much of

83

A horseman. That all came late:
  Suddenly, in your forties,
Learning to ride! A surrogate
  Virility, perhaps . . .

For me to think so could not
  Make you any more
Alive than you have been here,
  Open-necked cricket-shirt
And narrow head, behind
  The pricked ungainly ears
Of your white steed – all these
  Years, unnoticed mostly.

The Harrow

Unimaginable beings –
Our own dead friends, the dead
Notabilities, mourned and mourning,
Hallam and Tennyson . . . is it
Our loss of them that harrows?

Or is it not rather
Our loss of images for them?
The continued being of Claude
Simpson can be imagined.
We cannot imagine its mode.

Us too in this He harrows. It is not
Only on Easter Saturday
That it is harrowing
To think of Mother dead,
To think, and not to imagine.

He descended into –
Not into Hell but
Into the field of the dead
Where he roughs them up like a tractor
Dragging its tray of links.

Up and down the field, a tender bruising,
A rolling rug of iron, for the dead
Them also, the Virtuous Pagans
And others, He came, He comes
On Easter Saturday and

Not only then He comes
Harrowing them – that they,
In case they doubted it, may
Quicken and in more
Than our stale memories stir.

The Departed

They see his face!

Live in the light of . . .

Such shadows as they must
cast, sharp-edged;
the whole floor, said to be crystal,
barry with them. And long!

Spokes that reach even to us,
pinned as we are to the rim.

Rousseau in His Day

So many nights the solitary lamp had burned;
So many nights his lone mind, slowing down
Deliberately, had questioned, as it turned
Mooning upon its drying stem, what arc
Over a lifetime day had moved him through.

Always he hoped he might deserve a Plutarch,
Not to be one posterity forgot.
Nor have we. He has left his mark: one tight
Inched-around circuit of the screw of light,
As glowing shadows track the life of roses
Over unchosen soil-crumbs. It was not
What he'd expected or the world supposes.

After the Calamitous Convoy (July 1942)

An island cast
its shadow across
the water. Where
they sat upon
the Arctic shore
it shadowed them.

The mainland rose
tawny before
their eyes and closed
round them in capes
the island must
have slid from, once.

Under one horn
of land not quite
naked, above

the anchorage
white masonry
massed round a square.

From there one gained
the waterfront
by, they perceived,
a wooden stair
that wound down through
workshops and godowns.

Admiringly
their eyes explored
make-do-and-mend:
arrangements that
the earth lent – stairs,
cabins on struts,

stages of raised
catwalks between
stair and railed stair,
staked angles, ramps
and landings in
the open air.

Roof of the world,
not ceiling. One
hung to it not
as flies do but
as steeplejacks
move over rungs.

Survivors off
the Russian run,
years later they
believed the one
stable terrain
that Arctic one.

Seeing Her Leave

"gardens bare and Greek" – *Yvor Winters*

This West! this ocean! The bare
Beaches, the stony creek
That no human affair
Has soiled . . . Yes, it is Greek,

What she saw as the plane
Lifted from San Jose.
Under the shadow of Wren
She walks her ward today;

Once more my tall young woman
Has nerved herself to abandon
This Greece for the Graeco-Roman
Peristyles of London,

Where the archaic, the heated,
Dishevelled and frantic Greek
Has been planed and bevelled, fitted
To the civic, the moralistic.

And that has been noble, I think,
In her and others. Such
Centuries, sweat, and ink
Spent to achieve that much!

Lloyds of London, some
Indemnity for our daughters!
Those who trust the dome
Of St Paul's to the waters . . .

So much of the price is missed
In the tally of toil, ink, years;
Count, neo-classicist,
The choking back of tears.   (*California*)

Portland

after Pasternak

Portland, the Isle of Portland – how I love
Not the place, its name! It is as if
These names were your name, and the cliff, the breaking
Of waves along a reach of tumbled stone
Were a configuration of your own
Firm slopes and curves – your clavicles, your shoulder.
A glimpse of that can set the hallway shaking.

And I am a night sky that is tired of shining,
Tired of its own hard brilliance, and I sink.

Tomorrow morning, grateful, I shall seem
Keen, but be less clear-headed than I think;
A brightness more than clarity will sail
Off lips that vapour formulations, make
Clear sound, full rhyme, and rational order take
Account of a dream, a sighing cry, a moan.

Like foam on all three sides at midnight lighting
Up, far off, a seaward jut of stone.

Ars Poetica

in memoriam Michael Ayrton, sculptor

Walk quietly around in
A space cleared for the purpose.

Most poems, or the best,
Describe their own birth, and this
Is what they are – a space
Cleared to walk around in.

Their various symmetries are
Guarantees that the space has
Boundaries, and beyond them
The turbulence it was cleared from.

Small clearances, small poems;
Unlikely now the enormous
Louring, resonant spaces
Carved out by a Virgil.

The old man likes to sit
Here, in his black-tiled *loggia*
A patch of sun, and to muse
On Pasternak, Michael Ayrton.

Ayrton, he remembers.
Soon after reading his
Obituary, behold!
A vision of him:

The bearded, heavy-shouldered
London clubman, smiling
Against a *quattrocento*
View of the upper Arno.

This was in answer to prayer:
A pledge, a sufficient solace.
Poor rhyme, and are you there?
Bless Michael with your promise.

The old man likes to look
Out on his tiny *cortile*,
A flask of "Yosemite Road"
Cheap Chablis at his elbow.   (*California*)

90

In the Stopping Train

I have got into the slow train
again. I made the mistake
knowing what I was doing,
knowing who had to be punished.

I know who has to be punished:
the man going mad inside me;
whether I am fleeing
from him or towards him.

This journey will punish the bastard:
he'll have his flowering gardens
to stare at through the hot window;
words like "laurel" won't help.

He abhors his fellows,
especially children; let there
not for pity's sake
be a crying child in the carriage.

So much for pity's sake.
The rest for the sake of justice:
torment him with his hatreds
and love of fictions.

The punishing slow pace
punishes also places along the line
for having, some of them, Norman
or Hanoverian stone-work:

his old familiars, his
exclusive prophylactics.
He'll stare his fill at their
emptiness on this journey.

Jonquil is a sweet word.
Is it a flowering bush?
Let him hopelessly wonder
for hours if perhaps he's seen it.

Has it a white and yellow
flower, the jonquil? Has it
a perfume? Oh his art could
always pretend it had.

He never needed to see,
not with his art to help him.
He never needed to use his
nose, except for language.

Torment him with his hatreds,
torment him with his false
loves. Torment him with time
that has disclosed their falsehood.

Time, the exquisite torment!
His future is a slow
and stopping train through places
whose names used to have virtue.

*

A stopping train, I thought,
was a train that was going to stop.
Why board it then, in the first place?

Oh no, they explained, it is stopping
and starting, stopping and starting.

How could it, they reasoned gently,
be always stopping unless
also it was always starting?

I saw the logic of that;
grown-ups were good at explaining.

Going to stop was the same
as stopping to go. What madness!
It made a sort of sense, though.

It's not, I explained, that I mind
getting to the end of the line.
Expresses have to do that.

No, they said. We see . . .
But do you? I said. It's not
the last stop that is bad . . .

No, they said, it's the last
start, the little one; yes,
the one that doesn't last.

Well, they said, you'll learn
all about that when you're older.

Of course they learned it first.
Oh naturally, yes.

*

The man in the stopping train
sees them along the highway

with a recklessness like breeding
passing and re-passing:
dormobile, Vauxhall, Volvo.

He is shrieking silently: "Rabbits!"
He abhors his fellows.
Yet even the meagre arts
of television can
restore them to him sometimes,

93

when the man in uniform faces
the unrelenting camera
with a bewildered fierceness
beside the burnt-out Simca.

*

What's all this about flowers?
They have an importance he can't
explain, or else their names have.

Spring, he says, "stirs". It is what
he has learned to say, he can say
nothing but what he has learned.

And Spring, he knows, means flowers.
Already he observes this.
Some people claim to love them.

Love *them*? Love flowers? Love,
love . . . the word is hopeless:
gratitude, maybe, pity . . .

Pitiful, the flowers.
He turns that around in his head:
what on earth can it mean?

Flowers, it seems, are important.
And he can name them all,
identify hardly any.

*

The things he has been spared . . .
"Gross egotist!" Why don't
his wife, his daughter, shrill
that in his face?

94

Love and pity seem
the likeliest explanations;
another occurs to him –
despair too would be quiet.

*

Time and again he gave battle,
furious, mostly effective;
nobody counts the wear
and tear of rebuttal.

Time and again he rose
to the flagrantly offered occasion;
nobody's hanged for a slow
murder by provocation.

Time and again he applauded
the stand he had taken; how much
it mattered, or to what
assize, is not recorded.

Time and again he hardened
his heart and his perceptions;
nobody knows just how
truths turn into deceptions.

Time and again, oh time and
that stopping train!
Who knows when it comes to a stand,
and will not start again?

*

(*Son et Lumière*)
I have travelled with him many times
now. Already we nod,
we are almost on speaking terms.

95

Once I thought that he sketched
an apologetic gesture
at what we turned away from.

Apologies won't help him:
his spectacles flared like paired
lamps as he turned his head.

I knew they had been ranging,
paired eyes like mine,
igniting and occluding

coppice and crisp chateau,
thatched corner, spray of leaf,
curved street, a swell of furrows,

where still the irrelevant vales
were flowering, and the still
silver rivers slid west.

*

The dance of words
is a circling prison, thought
the passenger staring through
the hot unmoving pane
of boredom. It is not
thank God a dancing pain,
he thought, though it starts to jig
now. (The train is moving.) "This",
he thought in rising panic
(Sit down! Sit down!)
"this much I can command,
exclude. Dulled words, keep still!
Be the inadequate, cloddish
despair of me!" No good:
they danced, as the smiling land
fled past the pane, the pun's
galvanized *tarantelle*.

"A shared humanity . . ." He
pummels his temples. "Surely,
surely that means something."

He knew too few in love,
too few in love.

That sort of foolish beard
masks an uncertain mouth.
And so it proved: he took
some weird girl off to a weird
commune, clutching at youth.

Dear reader, this is not
our chap, but another.
Catch our clean-shaven hero
tied up in such a knot?
A cause of so much bother?

He knew too few in love.

Seur, near Blois

That a toss of wheat-ears lapping
Church-walls should placate us
Is easy to understand
In the abstract. That in fact
The instance of seeing also
A well with its wrought-iron stanchion,
Of feeling a balmy coolness,
Of hearing a Sunday noon silence,
Of smelling the six ragged lime-trees,
A church-door avenue, should

Placate, compose, is as much
As to say that the eye and the nose,
Also the ear and the very
Surface of one's skin is
An ethical organ; and further,
If indeed it is further
Or even other, a learned
Historian of man's culture.

Morning

Rose late: the jarring and whining
Of the parked cars under my windows, their batteries drained,
Somehow was spared. When I let out our schoolboy
Into the street, it was light: the place was alive and scented.

Spared too, for the most part, the puzzling tremulousness
That afflicts me often, these mornings. (I think
Either I need, so early, the day's first drink or
This is what a sense of sin amounts to:
Aghast incredulity at the continued success
Of an impersonation, the front put on to the world,
The responsibilities . . .)
                                    Let all that go:
Better things throng these nondescript, barged-through streets
(The sun! The February sun, so happily far and hazy . . .)
Than a mill of ideas.
                                    Sin, I will say, comes awake
With all the other energies, even at last the spark
Leaps on the sluggard battery, and one should have
Prosopopoeia everywhere: Stout Labour
Gets up with his pipe in his mouth or lighting
The day's first *Gauloise-filtre*; then stout
Caffeine like a fierce masseur
Rams him abreast of the day; stout Sin

Is properly a-tremble; stout
Vociferous Electricity chokes and chokes,
Stumbles at last into coughings, and will soon
Come to the door with a telegram – "Operation
Some Day This Week"; and stout
Love gets up out of rumpled sheets and goes singing
Under his breath to the supermarket, the classroom,
The briskly unhooded
Bureaucratic typewriter. See how
Sol winks upon its clever keys, and Flora
In a northern winter, far underground,
Feels herself sore at nubs and nipples.

And that mob of ideas? Don't knock them. The sick pell-mell
Goes by the handsome Olympian name of Reason.

To a Teacher of French

Sir, you were a credit to whatever
Ungrateful slate-blue skies west of the Severn
Hounded you out to us. With white, cropped head,
Small and composed, and clean as a Descartes
From as it might be Dowlais, "Fiery" Evans
We knew you as. You drilled and tightly lipped
Le futur parfait dans le passé like
The Welsh Guards in St James's, your pretence
Of smouldering rage an able sergeant-major's.

We jumped to it all right whenever each
Taut smiling question fixed us. Then it came:
Crash! The ferrule smashed down on the first
Desk of the file. You whispered: *Quelle bêtise!*
Ecoutez, s'il vous plait, de quelle bêtise
On est capable!
                    Yet you never spoke

99

To us of poetry; it was purely language,
The lovely logic of its tenses and
Its accidence that, mutilated, moved you
To rage or outrage that I think was not
At all times simulated. It would never
Do in our days, dominie, to lose
Or seem to lose your temper. And besides
Grammarians are a dying kind, the day
Of histrionic pedagogy's over.

You never taught me Ronsard, no one did,
But you gave me his language. He addressed
The man who taught him Greek as *Toi qui dores*
(His name was Jean Dorat) *la France de l'or*.
I couldn't turn a phrase like that on "Evans";
And yet you gild or burnish something as,
At fifty in the humidity of Touraine,
Time and again I profit by your angers.

Grudging Respect

As when a ruined face
Lifted among those crowding
For the young squire's largesse
Perceives him recognize
Her and she grabs, not for any
Languidly lofted penny
They scrabble for, but for his eyes
And pockets them, their clouding
That instant; and the abruptness
With which his obliging is checked,
His suddenly leaving the place . . .

Just so may a grudging respect
Be, from a despised one,
Not just better than none
At all, but sweeter than any.

A Spring Song

"stooped to truth and moralized his song"

Spring pricks a little. I get out the maps.
Time to demoralize my song, high time.
Vernal a little. *Primavera*. First
Green, first truth and last.
High time, high time.

A high old time we had of it last summer?
I overstate. But getting out the maps . . .
Look! Up the valley of the Brenne,
Louise de la Vallière . . . Syntax collapses.
High time for that, high time.

To Château-Renault, the tannery town whose marquis
Rooke and James Butler whipped in Vigo Bay
Or so the song says, an amoral song
Like Ronsard's where we go today
Perhaps, perhaps tomorrow.

Tomorrow and tomorrow and . . . Get well!
Philip's black-sailed familiar, avaunt
Or some word as ridiculous, the whole
Diction kit begins to fall apart.
High time it did, high time.

High time and a long time yet, my love!
Get out that blessed map.
Ageing, you take your glasses off to read it.
Stooping to truth, we potter to Montoire.
High time, my love. High time and a long time yet.

Wild Boar Clough

I.

A poet's lie!
        The boarhound and the boar
Do not pursue their pattern as before.
What English eyes since Dryden's thought to scan
Our spinneys for the Presbyterian,
The tusked, the native beast inflamed to find
And rend the spotted or the milk-white hind,
The true Church, or the half-true? Long ago
Where once were tusks, neat fangs began to grow;
Citizen of the World and Friend to Man,
The presbyter's humanitarian.
The poor pig learned to flute: the brute was moved
By plaudits of a conscience self-approved;
"Self in benevolence absorb'd and lost"
Absorbed a ruinous Redemption's cost.

This too a lie; a newer zealot's, worse
Than any poet's in or out of verse.
These were the hunting-calls, and this the hound,
Harried the last brave pig from English ground;
Now ermine, whited weasel, sinks his tooth
Deeper than wolf or boar into the Truth.
Extinct, the English boar; he leaves a lack.
Hearts of the disinherited grow black.

II.

When he grew up
in the England of silver
cigarette cases and
Baptist chapel on Sundays,

long white flannels were still
worn, and the Mission Fields
ripe for the scything Gospel
cost him a weekly penny.

The missionary box!
It rattled as he knocked it,
crouching near the wireless:
deuce, Fred Perry serving . . .

Doggedly he applies
himself to the exhumations:
these pre-war amateurs,
that missionary martyr.

As gone as Cincinnatus!
Still tongue-in-cheek revered, as
Republican virtue by
a silver-tongued florid Empire,

tired of that even, lately.

III.

To Loughwood Meeting House,
Redeemed since and re-faced,
Once persecuted Baptists
Came across sixty miles
Of Devon. Now we ask
Our own good wincing taste
To show the way to Heaven.

But if under clear-glassed windows,
The clear day looking in,
We should be always at worship
And trusting in His merits
Who saves us from the pathos
Of history, and our fears
Of natural disasters,

What antiquarian ferrets
We have been! As idle
An excrescence as Ionic
Pilasters would be, or
Surely the Puritan poet:
Burning, redundant candle,
Invisible at noon.

We are, in our way, at worship;
Though in the long-deflowered
Dissenting chapel that
England is, the slim
Flame of imagination,
Asymmetrical, wavers,
Starving for dim rose-windows.

IV.

And so he raged exceedingly,
excessively indeed, he raged excessively
and is said to have been drunk, as certainly
in some sense and as usual he was;
lacking as usual, and in some
exorbitant measure, charity,
candour in an old sense. How
a black heart learns white-heartedness, you tell me!

Raged, and beshrewed his audience of one
without much or at all
intending it, having his eyes not on
her but on the thing to be hunted down;

or so he will excuse himself, without
much confidence. The rapist's plea:
not her but womankind. He has
the oddest wish for some way to disgrace himself.

How else can a pharisee clear the accounts, and live?

V.

Wild Boar Clough . . . known to his later boyhood
    As the last gruelling stage before,
Feet and collar-bones raw, the tarmacadam
    Past unbelievable spa-hotels
Burned to the train at Buxton. Julian Symons,
    His poems, *Confessions of X*, reviewed
In *Poetry London*, bought on Buxton Station . . .

A nut-brown maid whom he cannot remember
    Sold him herb beer, a farmhouse brew,
One day above Wild Boar Clough, whose peat-sieved brown
    Waters were flecked below them. Legs
Were strong then, heart was light, was white, his swart
    Limbs where the old glad Adam in him,
Lissom and slim, exulted, carried him.

Somewhere that boy still swings to the trudging rhythm,
    In some brown pool that girl still reaches
A lazy arm. The harm that history does us
    Is grievous but not final. As
The wild boar still in our imaginations
    Snouts in the bracken, outward is
One steep direction gleefully always open.

So Lud's Church hides in Cheshire thereabouts
    Cleft in the moor. The slaughtered saints
Cut down of a Sunday morning by dragoons
    Grounded the English Covenant
In ling and peat-moss. Sound of singing drifts
    Tossed up like spume, persistently
Pulsing through history and out of it.

The Battered Wife

She thinks she was hurt this summer
More than ever before,
Beyond what there is cure for.

He has failed her once too often:
Once, it turns out, more
Than she had bargained for

In a bargain that of course
Nobody ever struck!
Oh, she had trusted her luck

Not once too often, but
All along the line:
And even this last time,

This summer, when reduced
To surely the bone her hope

Was just to live it through, his
Incalculable enmity
Rose up and struck. That he

Could no more calculate
Nor understand it than
She can, absolves the man

For the first time no longer. He
Will come back, she knows. She dreads it yet
Hopes for it, his coming back. A planet

Or else a meteor curves at the extreme
Bend of its vector, vehicle of
Prodigy and plague, and hopeless love.

G.M.B.
(10.7.77)

Old oak, old timber, sunk and rooted
    In the organic cancer
Of Devon soil, the need she had
    You could not answer.

Old wash and wump, the narrow seas
    Mindlessly breaking
She scanned lifelong; and yet the tide
    There's no mistaking

She mistook. She never thought,
    It seems, that the soft thunder
She heard nearby, the pluck and slide,
    Might tow her under.

I have as much to do with the dead
    And dying, as with the living
Nowadays; and failing them is
    Past forgiving.

Short Run to Camborne

The hideousness of the inland spine of Cornwall!
Redeemed (for of course in the long run all,
All is redeemed), but Wesley's chapels and all
In the slipstream of our short run rock rock to their fall.

And we surge on for Camborne, cheapness cheapened
By our going by as, with wreaths to honour the end
Of one who endured this cheapness, with our reeking
Put-put exhaust we exhaust the peace we are seeking.

107

Cheapness of granite-chips on the oil-starred road above Looe;
Our wanderings from the Wesleys and (it's true)
Dear-bought though they were, heaven-sent, their wanderings
    too . . .
Surge, surge we may but stray is all we do.

The spinelessness of the rock-ribbed once! The riven
Granite of Wesley's gospel that all are forgiven
Since all are redeemed . . . The loose shale slides and shelves
As we forgive each other and ourselves.

All are forgiven, or may be. But we owe
This much to our dead sister (at Polperro
Pixies and trivia . . .): humanly we know
Some things are unforgivable, even so.

The Admiral to His Lady

With you to Bideford,
Too old for stomaching
Rebuffs, not soon deterred
Nor often crossed of late,
I boomed along, not brooking
    The sky's mandate.

Habits of testy command
Forgot to say "weather permitting".
Though gales had rocked the land
And us, early and late,
There I was, squalls intermitting,
    Still hectoring fate.

Yet rained on, shoulders bowed,
Colour too high, too florid
In manner, voice too loud,
I felt like a youngster with you
That day, as wet winds flurried
        Torridge askew.

Wrecked body, barque of your wrecked
Hopes, or some of them – bitter
Reflections? . . . Harbours reflect
The changefulness of skies;
Bideford's waters glitter
        Like your hurt eyes.

Still, as the afterskirts
Of one black patch streel over
I brew up the next. It hurts
Each time a little less;
To cope with a demon lover
        Learn carelessness.

That rocking, jaunty way
You have, like Torridge's waters
Dancing into the bay . . .
You know what serves your turn;
You have, of all Eve's daughters,
        The least to learn!

Screech-Owl

I had to assure myself:
What it seemed I heard . . .
Was it my own stale self
Exhaled, or was it a bird?

Therefore with pride and relief,
Half-awake, coughing in bed,
I assure myself that screech
Came from outside my head.

Not the disgusting pipe of
Mucus lees that are
Replenishing the soon
Choked chambers of catarrh,

Not snore I heard, nor wheeze,
But something out of phase
With all of me: an owl
Out over Livingshayes.

In fact the birdcalls I
Can name are precious few.
Nightingales sang to me
Once, and I never knew.

Woodpigeon, meadowlark
With coo and trill augment
A gamut that remains
Indubitably scant.

And if, now I remember,
I lifted my head out of books
Enough to know one other
Call out of England: rooks . . .,

Is it not crows I mean
Or, what I am told is rare,
The death-conveying raven's
Croak through leaden air?

Bowels, adenoids,
Bald logic, brazen tongue . . .
Where is the other song the
Blackcap and wren have sung?

Cuckoo, plover, and owl:
A perilously confined
Aviary of sound for
One bedridden, or blind.

Grace in the Fore Street
for Roy Gottfried

You saw the sunlight ripen upon the wall,
Inching daily as the year wore full.

Behind you as you worked at Shakespeare rose,
Slovenly shelved, the job-lot of my books

An image of my randomness. Across them
A bush in the yard on a fine cold morning throws

Calendared shadows wavering over Bishop
Wilson's Maxims, and Calvin excerpted in French:

One late lunge after piety; and one
Long ago at face-saving erudition.

Which motive, or what other one, procured
The Psalms of David in Arthur Golding's version

I wish I knew, and knew what price to put on
"The fear of the Lord is clean, and endureth for ever."

I imagine you or another American friend
Explaining of me, when dead: "Now in his day

As an Englishman . . ." But not my Englishness
Nor anything else about me ever ripened.

The English year revolves and brings to leaf
Great ancient oaks which then unleaf themselves;

In which there is no consolation nor,
The scale at best but saecular, grounds for hope.

A better hope let me from my unkempt
Bruised library bestow on you. It goes:

> "Who can understand his faults?
> Cleanse me from my secret faults . . ."

Unearned composures have been known to enter
A place of unfirm purpose and fleet shadows.

Ox-Bow

> The time is at an end.
>   The river swirled
> Into an ox-bow bend, but now
>   It shudders and re-unites:
>   Adversary! Friend!

>   Adverse currents drove
>   This pair apart.
> A twin tormented throe embraced,
>   Enisled between them, one
>   Quadrant of earth, one grove.

Now for each other they yearn
    Across the eyot
That the peculiar flow of each
    Carved out, determined. Now,
    Now to each other they turn,

    And it is past belief
      That once they forked;
Or that, upstream and bypassed, trees
    Mirrored in mid-reach still
    Break into annual leaf.

No Epitaph

No moss nor mottle stains
My parents' unmarked grave;
My word on them remains
Stouter than stone, you told me.

"Martyred to words", you have thought,
Should be your epitaph;
At other times you fought
My self-reproaches down.

Though bitterly once or twice
You have reproached me with how
Everything ended in words,
We both know better now:

You understand, I shall not
If I survive you care
To raise a headstone for
You I have carved on air.

113

A Liverpool Epistle

to J.A. Steers, Esq, author of
"The Coastline of England and Wales"

Alfred, this couple here –
My son, your daughter – are
Can we deny it? strangers
To both of us. Ageing, I
Find I take many a leaf
Out of the useful book
Of your behaviour. "Prof.",
Your title for years, becomes
Me, or meets my need;
Mask for what heartaches, what
Uncertain, instantaneous
(Panicky sometimes)
Judgments how to behave in
This net we seem to have woven
Between us, or been caught in.

Under a rusty gown not
Actual but conjured
By our behaviour, what
In some diminished sense
Compromising situations we
Either escape, or handle! Still,
Today I was found at a loss,
Confronted with the local
University's stalwarts
Of a past age: Bernard Pares,
Oliver Elton, George
Sampson, Fitzmaurice-Kelly . . .
Not that they did not deserve
Attention, there in their daubed
Likenesses; but how?
What was required of "the Prof."?

In the event I managed
Well enough by my
Lenient expectations, but
I had such a sense of how
Tragical, one might say,
Our occupation is
Or may be. How
Beset it is, after all,
How very far from "secluded",
This life of the scholar my son
And your daughter have followed us into!

It was explained to me,
For instance, there was one
Liverpool professor
Had had to be painted out
Of the group-portrait: Kuno
Meyer, Professor of German,
Whose notable devotion
To Ancient Irish took,
Come 1914, rather
A different colour. He
Declared himself for his Kaiser
Belligerently. And I
Must admit I am baffled:
Passion also has its
Claims upon us, surely;
Even the sort that is called,
Smirkingly, "patriotic".

Kenneth Allott, a poet
I think you will not have read,
Gave us ("I give you", he wrote)
"The riotous gulls and the men
Crumpled, hat-clutching, in the wind's
Rages, and the shifting river",
Giving us Liverpool. Here
Anyone must be prompted

115

To solemn reflections in
A wind that must seem like the wind
Of history, blowing the chemical
Reek out of Runcorn over
The eerily unfrequented,
Once so populous, Mersey.

Cold hearth of empire, whose
Rasping cinders bring
Our erudite concerns
Home to us, with such
Asperity! This is
Liverpool, one enormous
Image of dereliction
Where yet our children warm themselves
And so warm us. We too
Are netted into it – you
Known as the protector
Of England's coastline, and
I, supposedly
Custodian of that other
Line around England: verse.

This turns, of course. Yes, one
Verse-line turns into the next
As Rodney Street into a slum, or
Philologists into Prussians;
Turnings in time as your
Headlands and bays are turnings
In space. A bittersweet pleasure
At best one takes in these
Revolutions, reversals,
Verses, whereas
The veerings of a coastline
(Seen from a lowflying aircraft,
A coastal road or, best,
A coasting ship) must be
Experienced, I think, as
A solemn sweetness always.

116

As prose at its saddest is less
Sorrowful than verse is
Necessarily, so
Geography, I have long
Thought, must be a sweeter
Study than history; sweeter
Because less cordial, less
Of heartbreak in it. More
Human warmth, it follows,
Is possible or common
In Liverpool than in
Some spick-and-span, intact,
Still affluent city. So
The warmth of our children's household
For the time being persuades me.

Two from Ireland

(1) *1969*, Ireland of the Bombers

Blackbird of Derrycairn,
Sing no more for me.
Wet fields of Dromahair
No more I'll see

Nor, Manorhamilton,
Break through a hazelwood
In tufted Leitrim ever.
That's gone for good.

Dublin, young manhood's ground,
Never more I'll roam;
Stiffly I call my strayed
Affections home.

Blackbird of Derrycairn,
Irish song, farewell.
Bombed innocents could not
Sing half so well.

Green Leinster, do not weep
For me, since we must part;
Dry eyes I pledge to thee,
And empty heart.

(2) *1977*, Near Mullingar
for Augustine Martin

"Green Leinster, never weep
    For me, since we must part.
Dry eyes I pledge to thee,
    And empty heart."

Travelling by train
    – For I am a travelling man –
Across fields that I laid
    Under this private ban,

I thought: a travelling man
    Will come and go, here now
And gone tomorrow, and
    He cannot keep a vow.

Forsworn, coming to Sligo
    To mend my battered past,
I thought: it must be true;
    The solder cannot last.

But, dear friends, I could weep.
    Is it the bombs have made
Old lesions knit, old chills
    Warm, and old ghosts be laid?

Atrociously, such changes!
　　The winning gentleness
Gentler still, and even
　　The poets not so reckless.

Twenty-five years at least
　　Higher up the slope
That England plunges down:
　　That much ground for hope.

Easy pronouncements from
　　The stranger, as he leaves!
The truth is, he was home
　　– Or so he half-believes.

Devil on Ice

Called out on Christmas Eve for a working-party,
Barging and cursing, carting the wardroom's gin
To save us all from sin and shame, through snow,
The night unclear, the temperature sub-zero,
　　　　　　　Oh I was a bombardier
　　　　　　　　　For any one's Angry Brigade
That Christmas more than thirty years ago!

Later, among us bawling beasts was born
The holy babe, and lordling Lucifer
With him alas, that blessed morn. And so
Easy it was, I recognize and know
　　　　　　　Myself the mutineer
　　　　　　　　　Whose own stale bawdry helped
Salute the happy morn, those years ago.

Red Army Faction could have had me then;
Not an intrepid operative, but glib,
A character-assassin primed to go,
Ripe for the irreplaceable though low
                    Office of pamphleteer.
                    Father of lies, I knew
My plausible sire, those Christmases ago.

For years now I have been amenable,
Equable, a friend of law and order,
Devil on ice. Comes Christmas Eve . . . and lo!
A babe we laud in baby-talk. His foe
                    And ours, not quite his peer
                    But his antagonist,
Hisses and walks on ice, as long ago.

Advent

Some I perceive, content
And stable in themselves
And in their place, on whom
One that I know casts doubt;
Knowing himself of those
No sooner settled in
Than itching to get out.

I hear and partly know
Of others, fearless and
Flinging out, whom one
I know tries to despise;
Knowing himself of those
No sooner loosed than they
Weeping sue for the leash.

Some I see live snug,
Embosomed. One I know
Maunders, is mutinous,
Is never loved enough;
Being of those who are
No sooner safely lodged
They chafe at cherishing.

Some I know who seem
Always in keeping, whom
One I know better blusters
He will not emulate;
Being of those who keep
At Advent, Whitsuntide,
And Harvest Home in Lent.

Some who are his kin
Have strewn the expectant floor
With rushes, long before
The striding shadow grows
And grows above them; he,
The deeper the hush settles,
Bustles about more business.

The eclipse draws near as he
Scuttles from patch to shrinking
Patch of the wintry light,
Chattering, gnashing, not
Oh not to be forced to his knees
By One who, turned to, brings
All quietness and ease.

Self-contradictions, I
Have heard, do not bewilder
That providential care.
Switch and reverse as he
Will, this one I know,
One whose need meets his
Prevents him everywhere.

Having No Ear

Having no ear, I hear
And do not hear the piano-tuner ping,
Ping, ping one string beneath me here, where I
Ping-ping one string of Caroline English to
Tell if Edward Taylor tells
The truth, or no.

Dear God, such gratitude
As I owe thee for giving, in default
Of a true ear or of true holiness,
This trained and special gift of knowing when
Religious poets speak themselves to God,
And when, to men.

The preternatural! I know it when
This perfect stranger – angel-artisan –
Knows how to edge our English Upright through
Approximations back to rectitude,
Wooing it back through quarter-tone
On quarter-tone, to true.

Mystical? I abjure the word, for if
Such faculty is known and recognized
As may tell sharp from flat, and both from true,
And I lack that capacity, why should I
Think Paradise by other light than day
Sparkled in Taylor's eye?

Siloam

for Clyde Binfield
"By cool Siloam's shady rill" *(Heber)*

Arkansaw's westernmost county
Is dry; we nip back over
The out-of-town stateline for
Liquor in Oklahoma.

In the next one, "wet", a drive-in
Announces "Kinky Ladies",
A shack says "Modern Massage",
Not open yet for trading.

A titter: "This is what
Free Churchmen mean by a *felt
Religion*? We are, are we not,
At the heart of the Bible Belt?"

We are. This is Siloam
Springs. Once off the highway,
We walk in the 1930s,
Provincial yesterday:

The two or three blocks we walk
Of dark-brick downtown, sparsely
Frequented, could be almost
How I remember Barnsley,

Except for this river, whatever
River it is, scarved round
The whole small so-called "city",
Flowing without a sound.

Green, deep-bushed green, the waters
And weir under the hill;
A little park by cool
Siloam's shady rill

Recalls in bronze the appalling
Highest the waters rose
Once, and the devastation –
By God's will, we suppose.

Imagine a deacon of
Drowned bottomlands, his brows
Sternly, despairingly knitted,
In the next county's whorehouse

Drowning himself! This country
Was lately and not completely
Humanized; here the dooms
Come suddenly and stately.

It is thus I perceive this lady,
Hatted and gloved, advancing,
Two grandchildren in tow,
Her eyes on us bright and dancing.

And this is on the bridge
Under the hanging wood,
Feeling precarious over
Siloam's fateful flood.